TITUS
Living As God's Very Own People

UNDERSTANDING THE BOOK

TITUS

LIVING AS GOD'S VERY OWN PEOPLE

STUART BRISCOE

Harold Shaw Publishers
Wheaton, Illinois

ISBN 0-87788-813-2

Cover design by David LaPlaca

Library of Congress Cataloging-in-Publication Data

Briscoe, Stuart.
    Titus : living as God's very own people / Stuart Briscoe.
      p.   cm. — (Understanding the Book)
    Includes bibliographical references.
    ISBN 0-87788-813-2
    1. Bible. N.T. Titus—Criticism, interpretation, etc. I. Bible. N.T.
Titus. English. New International. 1994. II. Title. III. Title: Living
as God's very own people. IV. Series: Briscoe, Stuart
Understanding the Book series.
BS2755.2.B75 1994
227'.85077—dc20   94-2437
                                               CIP

99 98 97 96 95 94

10 9 8 7 6 5 4 3 2 1

Contents

Introduction

The Epistle to Titus is one of the shortest books of the Bible and, accordingly, has been somewhat overlooked. This is unfortunate, because despite its size, the depth and significance of its teaching cannot be overstated, and its relevance for today's church should not be underestimated.

Titus was one of the men into whom Paul had poured his life and with whom he had shared his ministry. Their relationship serves as a model for the sort of relationship that can and should develop between Christian leaders and the next generation, who will assume their mantles. All too often churches wither on the vine when those whom God used to start them leave the scene without adequate leadership to carry on the work. Where this is true the church of Jesus Christ is inevitably impoverished. Paul not only reminds us that those of the next generation are one of our best investments, but he also shows practically how to do the investing.

Today, with so many means of communication, there has come a proliferation of messages. It is not at all unusual for even the most well-meaning believers to become bogged down in confounding and controversial issues as they tune in to one preacher after another through books, tapes, radio, and television. Considerable maturity is required in both biblical knowledge and social skills to clear up the confusion. Paul recognized this truth in his ministry and instructed Titus to make solid teaching, practical application, and personalized training available to the people of the infant churches.

In short, Paul told Titus how to work in a church so that it would function well and become recognizable in the local environment as the people of God. While many pew packers have differing views of what the church is and, accordingly, what it is supposed to be doing, there are still many influential people in the pulpits and the pews who recognize the unique and noble position the local church fills in the plan and economy of God. In addition, they are deeply committed to work hard to see that, as much as it depends on them, God might be free to work in, with, and through them to the purifying of his people. This book was written by one who shares this concern.

1

Identifying God's People

Titus 1:1-5

At first sight the initial four verses of the apostle Paul's letter to Titus do not hold any great promise, because they're simply a traditional formal opening to a letter. In the days in which Paul was writing, it was customary for the writer first to introduce himself and, second, to state the person to whom he was writing, and then, to give formal traditional greetings. So Paul's Epistle fits into the traditional formal pattern.

But there is a difference. Paul takes all this traditional formality and invests it with a specific significance. For instance, he doesn't just say "Paul." He says, "Paul, a servant of God and an apostle of Jesus Christ," and goes on for three verses. He doesn't just say "Titus," the person to whom he's writing. But in a beautiful succinct statement he calls him "my true son in our common faith."

As far as the formal greetings are concerned, "grace and peace" were normal greetings; but you'll notice that Paul invests them with deep significance. For the grace and peace that he's talking about emanate "from God the Father and Christ Jesus our Savior."

So already we have the clue that this formal traditional greeting is something of deep importance.

The purpose of the letter is included, not in these four verses, but in the fifth one. Paul and Titus have been on an evangelistic mission to Crete. Paul moved on and wrote to Titus, explaining, "The reason I left you in Crete was that you might straighten out what was left unfinished and appoint elders in every town, as I directed you."

The apostle Paul was not just interested in evangelizing so that individuals could come to a personal relationship with Christ. That, of course, was the start. He was interested in taking these new converts and forming fellowships, churches, "in every town" in Crete.

Paul told Titus to "straighten out what was left unfinished," specifically to develop the structure of the church. To do this, Titus is given the responsibility to personally appoint elders in every town. So Titus's particular ministry is to pick up the fruits of evangelism, form them into bodies of believers in all the different towns all over Crete, and establish churches. It's what we call, in contemporary jargon, a church-planting ministry. It is, of course, a very important aspect of all ministry.

However, while the idea of straightening out what was left unfinished in appointing elders in every church is the human side of what was being done, Paul points out the divine aspect of what is going on. In Titus 2:14 he says, speaking of our Lord Jesus, that he "gave himself for us to redeem us from all wickedness and to purify for himself a people that are his very own, eager to do what is good."

When Titus goes to the different towns around Crete and establishes churches, that's the human side of it, the practical side. But the divine and spiritual side of it is that God is purifying a people that are his very own. Put those two things together and you'll discover something very important: The ministry of the gospel requires that when we bring people to Christ, we introduce them to a fellowship of believers that takes seriously the fact that they are to be God's very own people in their geographic locations.

We're going to examine this Epistle to find out what it really means not only to be related to Christ, but in that relationship to be related to those who are Christ's and to be a member of God's very own people in a specific geographic location.

In the introduction Paul says he is "a servant of God and an apostle of Jesus Christ for the faith of God's elect." Notice that little expression "God's elect." The word *elect* means "to choose," and Scripture shows quite clearly that God is in the habit of electing, or choosing. Whenever we think in terms of God's elect, we think of a people that God has called, a people he has chosen for himself. The basis of this is found in the Old Testament, where on numerous occasions we read of God choosing a people for himself.

God Chose Israel As His People

The Israelites were not chosen to be God's people because they were special; they were not chosen because they were perfect; they were not chosen because they were strong. They were chosen because they were chosen. In other words, the choice rests with God himself. But behind the choice of Israel as a people is another: God's choice to have a people at all. Why does he want a people in the first place? We might well ask that question when we remember the hassles God had with his people, Israel. But I think the answer is very important.

Why is God anxious to produce communities of people who are readily identifiable, in a special sense, as his people? We need to remember that in the beginning God created man. After he created man he left him for a little while and then decided man couldn't make it on his own. So God had a wonderful idea: He created woman.

When God created man he created an individual. As soon as God created woman, he created community, or society. Then disaster struck. Man fell, and community also began to fall apart. Man and woman had a beautiful relationship that promptly deteriorated. Not only that, they produced children: The first one they produced was a murderer, and the second was the brother he murdered. In other words, community—society—promptly began to disintegrate.

We know that God certainly cares about fallen man—so much that he sent Christ to be the Savior of fallen mankind. But does God care about fragmented society? Yes. He has ordained that those fallen men who are redeemed by Christ should be a part of an alternate society, a new, readily identifiable community. And that community, that alternate society, is called *the church,* the people of God, God's elect, those who are particularly his.

To model community

The first reason God chose a people was so that they might live as a model community in the midst of fragmentation to show what community is all about. He called Israel and made them a nation. Then he placed them as a nation and a people in the midst of other nations and said to them, "Okay, now show the nations how nations behave when God is the Lord."

To show his sovereign power

The second reason God chose a people for himself was that he wanted to make it very clear that he was the sovereign Lord, that he would act as he chose. And he demonstrated this on numerous occasions with his people. Their history is one long story of God's sovereign intervention in their affairs. Perhaps the best-known illustration is when they were brought out of Egypt in that massive exodus. In a remarkable way, God stretched forth his mighty arm and delivered them out of the hands of the Egyptians. Whenever you read about Israel's history, you will find that God's chosen people constantly refer to the Exodus as a sovereign act of God. It is a basic plank of their history, something that is deeply important to them.

To show his grace

Over and over again God dealt with his own in a way they didn't deserve. He showered his blessings upon them even when they were ungrateful, even when they were rebellious. For instance, in the wilderness he showers manna, bread from heaven, upon them on a daily basis. But they are a grumbling people: disgruntled, wishing they were back in Egypt, doubting their leadership, schismatic—just a nasty bunch of people. Yet God says, "I won't give you what you deserve; I'll give you the manna you don't deserve."

To show what it means to belong to him

Fourth, God chose a people in order that he might clearly identify the solemnity of being related to him.

Even though these people were his elect, even though he had chosen them to be his people, that didn't mean it all came about automatically. His people had all kinds of responsibilities, and he told them, "Either you do it my way, or you're in trouble." They didn't do it his way; they finished up in trouble. He warned them repeatedly through the prophets of the possibility of exile; they didn't heed his warning. The result? The elect people, the chosen people, demonstrated categorically that you don't mess around with God. Because they did not do it God's way, but followed their own paths, the chosen people did go into exile and were dispersed around the world—a consequence of their sin and disobedience.

So God had his elect people. He chose them so that, in his dealings with them, they might learn and teach other nations about God.

God Chose Christ As His Stone

Today God's elect people are the church. We are the chosen of God by virtue of our relationship with his Son, Jesus Christ. In 1 Peter 2:4 we read: "As you come to him [the Lord Jesus], the living Stone—rejected by men but chosen *[elect]* by God and precious to him—you also, like living stones, are being built into a spiritual house to be a holy priesthood."

Using the picture of Christ as the stone, the chosen one of God, Peter then shows how he is the cornerstone in verse 6, the capstone in verse 7, the stumbling stone in verse 8. Jesus was chosen by God to function in this capacity.

The *cornerstone* is the base upon which everything is built; the foundation. The *capstone* is the locking stone that makes everything hold together. The *stumbling stone* is that over which people trip if they don't treat it properly. This is what Christ was chosen to be. He was chosen to be the foundation of everything that God is doing for man. He was chosen to be the capstone who makes everything in God's dealings with man make sense and hold together. He is the foundation and the basis of everything God wants to do, if men will respond. But if they won't respond, they will find that he will be the one against whom they will bang their shins and skin their knees and bump their noses; they will stumble over him and find him an offense.

God Chose Us As His Church

In Ephesians 1:4 Paul talks about the church, the people of God. He talks about those who are in Christ: "For he [God] chose us in him before the creation of the world to be holy and blameless in his sight." These people who are the church, who are in Christ, who are the body of Christ, God also calls "the elect," the special people of God. God has chosen that the church in today's world should be his very own people. It is terribly important that believers understand the significance of the body of Christ and what it means to be in Christ.

Our problem is that we are individualized in our lives and in our thinking. This flows over into our spiritual experience, which often is on a limited, individualized basis. But that doesn't go far enough. We are to understand ourselves to be individuals related, not only to Christ, but to those related to Christ, God's elect people in that particular place, the church.

One of the problems many of us have is that we say what I used to say in my late teens and early twenties: "I'm all in favor of Jesus Christ, but as far as his church is concerned, forget it." I remember applauding with great enthusiasm when I saw a movie in which the young Cliff Richards was talking to the vicar of a church. This young kid said to the stereotypical English Anglican vicar: "If I was Jesus Christ and came back to earth and saw what you'd done to my church, I'd sue you." And I clapped with everybody else. We thought that was absolutely great, because it is the easiest thing in the world to knock the church. Anybody who can't knock the church has simply chloroformed his critical capabilities. Remember, the church is made up exclusively of sinners, so anybody who can't find fault with it just isn't trying.

But we don't have the freedom to casually criticize the church of Jesus Christ because it is a community of people in Christ, chosen of God, and placed in geographic locations to *be* something and to *do* something. This is our calling. It's a noble calling; it's a frightening calling. But it's our calling, nevertheless.

To glorify him

The apostle Paul says that those of us who are chosen in Christ are called "to the praise of his glorious grace" (Eph. 1:6). That doesn't mean we as *individuals* glorify him; it means that what we are as a *community* glorifies him. That's why, you see, it's such a hassle being part of the church of Jesus Christ. It is a tremendously demanding calling—not just individually to be to his glory, but collectively to act as a community, as a fellowship, in a way that glorifies him.

To do good

It isn't just what we are; it's also what we do. As we have already pointed out, Titus 2:14 says that the people who are his very own are eager to do what is good. We are a people characterized by what we are (to the praise of his glory) and what we do (that which is good by his standards of goodness).

So the apostle Paul sends Titus on a very simple mission. He says, "All right. Go into every town in Crete and establish churches there from the products of our evangelism. Ordain elders in every place and straighten out what needs to be straightened out. And always remember, Titus, as you are straightening out the practical details of these churches, you are making it possible for Christ to purify for himself his very own people in those towns."

What an exciting concept that, in every town in Crete, it will be possible to identify God's very own people. What an exciting thought to think that in your city or town today you can identify God's very own people. Wherever we go around the world we can identify God's very own people. That is what we are called to do. The church is not just a lot of individuals; it is a community of people knit together as the body of Christ, God's called people, his very own.

Do you understand the significance of what it means to be identified with Christ and then to identify with a church? If so, are you openly willing to commit yourself to his people? To throw your weight with that people so you can be to his glory, do what is good, and be clearly identifiable in your geographic location as a member of God's very own people? Or are you keeping your spiritual experience personal? Are you keeping yourself peripheral? Have you determined that as little involvement as possible is the way to go?

I remember somebody once telling me, when I said something about the church, "You've got to understand, Stuart, we aren't joiners; we never join anything." But, fortunately, they began to listen to Scripture and discovered that if you identify with Christ, you are called to identify with God's very own people.

What Are the People of God Like?

If these people are to be readily identifiable as such in a specific geographic location, it seems reasonable to ask, What are the characteristics of these people? What is it that helps identify them? Paul tells us in his formal, traditional, but expanded greeting that he is "a servant of God and an apostle of Jesus Christ" for three reasons: "for the faith of God's elect"; for "the knowledge of the truth that leads to godliness"; and for "the hope of eternal life, which God, who does not lie, promised before the beginning of time."

How do we identify the people of God? First, they're people of faith; second, they're people of knowledge; third, they are people of hope—and all these not just as individuals, but as a community.

People of faith
God's very own people are people of faith in the sense that they know what it is to be justified by faith. Everybody who believes in

God would like to be right with God eventually. A lot of people who believe in God want to delay it until as late as possible. They want to do their own thing and then get right with God at the last possible minute. But that simply shows how little they understand God.

People who are serious about God want to be right with God, and there are two basic ways they think they can do it. One is to "do your best and hope for the best." The problem with this concept is that everyone disagrees with what is best. There is a problem with the definition. If these people say you get right with God by doing your best, and you try to nail them down a bit, they'll say that keeping the Ten Commandments, living by the Sermon on the Mount, and following the Golden Rule are examples of "doing your best."

I have spent time talking with people who advocate these approaches, and I've noticed that none of them have ever been able to show me where in the Bible the Ten Commandments are; none of them could tell me which Gospel the Sermon on the Mount is in; and none of them could quote the Golden Rule. In other words, a lot of people who say the way you get right with God is by doing your best aren't really taking it seriously. If you try to do your best, hoping that it will make you right with God, number one, you won't do it, and number two, even if you did, it wouldn't be good enough.

The second way people think they can get right with God is not on the basis of doing their best and earning it, but in admitting that their best isn't good enough. They admit openly to the Lord, "I am unhealthy, inadequate, and a rebellious, sinful person. I deserve only your righteous indignation, but I understand that you offer graciously what I don't deserve, and I ask for this gracious provision and accept all you offer in grateful faith."

The people of faith are the people who don't talk a lot of nonsense about getting right with God by doing their best. The people of faith are those who say the only way you can get right with God is by asking him graciously to give them what they don't deserve, for Christ's sake, and then by faith receive it. It's what the Bible calls being justified by grace (Titus 3:7) through faith. The people of God, those who are God's very own people, know they have been justified by faith. That's why churches ask those who come to join if they can testify to the fact that they have been saved by grace through faith. If they can't, they haven't even started to be people of faith.

You start as a person of faith by being justified by faith, but then you go on from there. You live by faith. Dr. Carl Henry made a powerful statement: "A disconcertingly wide segment of American society succumbs to the premise that life has not come from God, does not move towards God, and cannot be enriched by God." That's basically the philosophy of our society.

We call ourselves a Christian nation; we talk about the founding fathers until we become blue in the face; we come up with all kinds of highfalutin statements about getting prayer back in the schools and whatnot. But what we're really confronting in this society is a wide segment of people who frankly don't believe that life came from God or is moving toward God or can be enriched by God; in other words, God is utterly irrelevant.

If that's the society as a whole, do you see how easy it is to be a person of faith and to stand out among them? If you believe by faith that you came from God and that you're going to God and are answerable to him, and you believe by faith that every single day God can intervene in your affairs by his Spirit, through his Word, and in the fellowship of believers that enriches your life, you will stick out like a sore thumb in this faithless generation.

Now, what is a community of believers? A community of believers is a visible, tangible body of believers in a specific situation, comprised of people of faith. Are you a person of faith? Have you been justified by faith? Do you get up in the morning and thank God that you've come from him and you are going to him and are living unto him? Do you open up your life to his intervention, reckon with his grace, count on his presence, and live in the life and the glory of his being? That's faith. God's very own people are people of faith.

People of knowledge

Second, God's very own people are people of knowledge. He says that they are the people who have "knowledge of the truth that leads to godliness." Knowledge of the truth means, first of all, that they have accumulated data. They have their facts right about the truth of God, or, to put it another way, they have taken time out to learn their theology.

One of the things that concerns me about the contemporary church in North America is that we are more experience-oriented than theology-oriented. For instance, if you look at the books people buy, you will find that a high percentage are experience-oriented books: How can I feel better? How can I look better? How can I sort my marriage out? How can I sort my kids out? How am I going to be or feel or look or do better?

Then look at how many people buy books of theology—on the person of God, the person of Christ, the person of the Holy Spirit, the theology of man, the theology of the last times, the theology of the church. You will discover that the wide majority of people in the Christian community don't study at all, and a wide selection of those who do study are committed exclusively to experience-oriented study.

People who really take time to get a knowledge of the truth are a small minority, and this is a concern. When the apostle Paul says that the people of God are people of knowledge, however, he is not just talking about people who know truth. He is talking about people who know truth to the point of acknowledging the truth. The Greek word he uses is *epignosis,* which means "to know thoroughly and to acknowledge what you know."

I know that Elizabeth is the queen of the United Kingdom. But if she were to walk into the room, the fact that I know her would not necessarily mean that I would behave properly towards her. I might just sit down, stick my hands in my pockets, chew my gum, and ignore her. I would know who she is, but I might not acknowledge who she is. If I were to acknowledge what I know, it would mean that I would stand up, quietly give attention to her, and treat her

11

with respect. It doesn't mean I have to agree with her policies; it doesn't mean I have to like her as a person; what it means is that she is the queen and I acknowledge her as such. It's one thing to know. It's another thing to acknowledge. *Epignosis,* the knowledge of which Paul speaks, is acknowledging the truth that we know. And the people of God are people of knowledge—they know the truth, and they are prepared to acknowledge in their lives the truth. These are the people of God, God's very own people.

But notice that Paul goes on to say that this knowledge of truth leads to godliness. The Greek word for "godliness" is *eusebeia,* which means literally "to tremble before God," or to treat him with deep respect and utter reverence, or, to use the old-term expression that was discarded long ago, to have a great fear of God. That's what godliness really means. Part of our problem is that we have become on such intimate, friendly terms with God that he's a bit of a buddy. It's rather nice to have that intimate relationship with God, and it's all valid, unless it brings us to the point of overlooking the fact that he is awesome.

A godly person is one who always has a sense of awe when he understands the majesty of God. A godly person comes always with a sense of trembling, because he knows that before the holiness of God man is utterly sinful himself. A person who is godly looks at the power of God and is overwhelmed by a sense of his own inadequacy. So, with a sense of awe, a sense of shame, and a sense of inadequacy, he comes humbly before his God with reverence and holy fear. That's what happens when you know and acknowledge the truth. It produces godliness.

God's very own people are people of faith and knowledge. Isaiah 66:2 sums this up magnificently. It says that the Lord esteems the person "who is humble and contrite in spirit, and trembles at my word." You members of the people of God are identified with a community of people that have a deep-down desire to be known in their towns as God's very own people: people of faith, people of knowledge.

People of hope

The apostle Paul goes on to say that he is a servant and an apostle for the "hope of eternal life, which God, who does not lie, promised before the beginning of time" (Titus 1:2). He is saying that those who are identified with the living God are people who are characterized by hope. That hope is an overwhelming confidence, and it relates to eternal life. They believe that when the Scriptures say these things are written "that you may know that you have eternal life" (1 John 5:13), they are written to be believed.

I remember talking to someone who said, "Do you think you have eternal life? Do you mean to stand there and tell me that you think you have eternal life?"

"Yes," I replied. "And I don't think it, I know it."

"I think you're arrogant."

I said, "I can understand that."

"Nobody, but nobody can know that they have eternal life," he claimed.

So I said, "Now I think you're arrogant."

"Why?"

"Because you presume to know better than the Word of God. The Word of God says that these things are written that you may *know* that you have eternal life. And you know better. Who's arrogant? Somebody who believes the Word of God or somebody who knows better than the Word does?"

It is not arrogance to put your trust in Christ, to come humbly and contritely before God and tremble at his Word, to admit that you can't save yourself, to come open-handed, empty-handed, and brokenhearted before God and say, "God, for Christ's sake, forgive me and give me what I don't deserve." That's not arrogance. That's common sense. And there are people who have come before the Lord and know that they have eternal life: this has become their hope, their confidence. Why? Because this eternal life was promised to them by a God who cannot and who does not lie.

Norman J. Clayton, in his great hymn "My Hope Is in the Lord" wrote these words: "for me he died, for me he lives, and everlasting life and light he freely gives." What does that mean for all God's people? It means that life down here is tinted with the glow of life up there. It means that eternity invests itself into all our experiences of time. It means that the most mundane things of earth are touched with the glory of heaven.

I'll tell you something very exciting. There are people who are full of hope and people who are full of knowledge. There are also people who are full of faith. When they get together, they become a church; they become an assembly; they become a visible, vital, viable entity in society—God's very own people.

I encourage you to be a part. One of the most crucial things that ever happened to me was when a good friend of mine, a very well-known preacher, said to me after hearing me preach one time, "Stuart, the problem with your theology is it incorporates no ecclesiology." In other words, he was telling me everything I had to say was related to an individual's relationship with God. "But," he said, "there's a whole lot more to theology than that. What about the individual's relationship to each other in the church, the community of believers?"

Ask yourself these questions: Do I take the church of Jesus Christ seriously? Have I identified with the people of God? Can they count on me? Do they even know who I am? Do they know my faith, my knowledge, my hope? Does my faith, knowledge, and hope engender faith, knowledge, and hope in others? Does the faith, knowledge, and hope of others encourage my faith, knowledge, and hope? Am I part of those whom others know are God's very own people? Or am I just going it alone, making sure that I'm as uninvolved as possible in what God is committed to—the building of his church?

Making It Real

1. For what four reasons did God choose a people to be his very own?

2. Why do you think people in our society are more committed to individual worship than to corporate worship?

3. In what three ways can we, as a church, be readily identifiable as God's people?

4. What is the significance of being identified with God's people in a particular location? How do you show your commitment to your particular church?

Overseeing God's People

Titus 1:6-9

*L*eadership is largely a catalyst for what happens in a corporate body. While many churches approach their ministry in different ways and have different emphases, worldwide studies show that a vital, virile church that is achieving what it appears God has called it to achieve has, without exception, a vital, virile leadership.

I think it's also true that where you have a fellowship that has weak leadership, you have a fellowship that is weak. Now that doesn't mean that leadership is everything, but leadership is a massive part of the health, well-being, effectiveness, and efficiency of a fellowship of believers. The leaders Titus was commissioned to identify were called elders.

What Are Elders?

We don't use the term *elder* very much in our everyday vocabulary. But it is a common word in biblical understanding, so let's be sure that we understand what Paul is getting at when he talks about the necessity for elders. Even though the word *elder* is used in verse 6, and *overseer* in verse 7 (your translation may say *bishop* or some other designation) they all refer to the same people.

The apostle Paul uses two different Greek words, and he uses them interchangeably. The first word is *presbuteros*. The second word is *episkopos*. These two words, while they are quite different, obviously refer to the same kind of people. So when we talk about "elder," "overseer," "bishop" or whatever English translation you are using, understand that we are talking about these two Greek words, *presbuteros* and *episkopos*.

Presbuteros

The word *presbuteros* is found in the Septuagint, the Greek translation of the Old Testament. Some of your Bibles may have in the margin or footnotes the symbol LXX. That is the Roman numeral 70, the symbol for the Septuagint. The original meaning of *presbuteros* is "old man" or "bearded one." My children affectionately call me old man (I hope affectionately), and, of course, I'm to understand that they're using the term very loosely. But *presbuteros* originally meant an old man or somebody who had a beard. If you go into many of the societies in the Eastern world today, you'll find that the old men always have beards. And if they are gray beards, they are symbols of dignity and maturity.

The first time I was in Bangladesh and met with a group of Muslim elders I couldn't understand why I was so warmly received. I was told afterwards it was purely because of my beard. The young missionary who took me there said, "I don't get anything like your reception among those people, even though I've been working among them for years." And he said, "I can't wait until I can grow a beard and see it turn white." The last time I saw him he had started working on his beard, but I'm afraid it was black and resembled five o'clock shadow.

The elders of the Bible (*presbuteros,* old men or bearded ones) were instrumental in many of the decisions that were made as the people of Israel came out of Egypt and wandered through the wilderness.

Moses is the one who gets all the credit. And he's the one who also gets all the blame. Moses is the one who gets all the publicity, but if you read carefully, you'll notice that there were many elders, many mature people, who were responsible for the leadership of the people of Israel. When the children of Israel eventually moved into the Promised Land they ceased to be nomadic and began to establish their towns. Whenever they established a town, they always had a group of elders who were the leaders of the city. And their responsibility was "to sit in the gate." That sounds a little strange to us, but it means that, among other things, they fulfilled a judicial function. All the disputes were brought to them. Sitting in the main entrance to the city, these elderly, bearded, mature, dignified people were the ones who handled the most awkward situations.

Later on in the development of the Jewish people, when the Sanhedrin was founded, certain members of the Sanhedrin were also called the elders. Eventually, after the destruction of Herod's temple and the scattering of the Jewish people throughout the world, if there were twelve Jewish males in any city, they were free to form a synagogue. If they formed a synagogue they had a governor, and the word for governor in the Greek was *presbuteros*.

When Paul, a Jew, along with other Jewish Christians went to the dispersed Jews, preached the gospel, and brought them to Christ, they established Christian churches. It's quite understandable that, from that background, they should immediately think in terms of a leadership that was called "elders." And I believe one of the reasons the apostle Paul returned to many areas of Asia Minor and established churches and appointed elders is simply because he realized this was a crucial, vital part of the spiritual experience.

Episkopos

The word *episkopos* was used commonly by the Greeks in a variety of ways. For instance, in Greek mythology some of the gods were called *episkopoi*. This doesn't mean that the gods were bishops. *Episkopos* means literally to "watch over," "look after," or "care for." So when they gave the title *episkopos* to one of their gods, the idea was that he was a caring, watching, overseeing god who was particularly concerned for a city, a people, or a country.

In the same way, the Greeks had government officials with the title *episkopos*. For instance, when the Greeks were able to overrun certain areas and subsidiary nations came under their control, they would send administrators to the various cities. The title for the administrator was *episkopos*. He was the person who was going to oversee. When the people of Israel came back from their captivity and restored Jerusalem, some of the leaders in that particular restoration period and some of the administrators of the rebuilding of Jerusalem were given the same title.

This term, therefore, came quite naturally into use in the new Christian fellowships, because as they were founded, they needed not only mature, dignified people of experience who could function in leadership roles, but also people who could administrate, oversee, care for, and be responsible for this community.

Why does the apostle Paul sometimes use *presbuteros* and other times *episkopos?* I will suggest just two answers. One is possibly that *presbuteros* was the word to describe the character of the elders, being characterized by maturity and dignity. But *episkopos* described their function rather than their character.

Another suggestion is that the Hebrew people, probably because of the Septuagint, would be more favorably disposed towards *presbuteros,* and those of the Greek background would probably understand more clearly the meaning of *episkopos*. Whatever the case, as Titus is given the job of ordaining elders in these areas, it's rather obvious that Paul, under the inspiration of the Holy Spirit, is saying that these churches need people who are characterized by dignity, maturity, and wisdom, and who are going to be seriously involved in overseeing, leading, and caring for this fellowship of believers.

Who are these people to be? I want to suggest, first of all, some general qualifications and then some specific qualities.

General Qualifications of Elders

Notice in Titus 1:6-9 (see also 1 Timothy 3) that the apostle maps out some of the general qualifications: "An elder must be blameless." That doesn't mean he has to be perfect, because it would rather narrow our choices, wouldn't it? "An elder must be blameless, the husband of but one wife, a man whose children believe and are not open to the charge of being wild and disobedient." Since an overseer is entrusted with God's work, he must be blameless—not overbearing, not quick-tempered, not given to drunkenness, not violent, not pursuing dishonest gain. Rather he must be hospitable, one who loves what is good, who is self-controlled, upright, holy and disciplined. He must hold firmly to the trustworthy message as it has been taught, so that he can encourage others by sound doctrine and refute those who oppose it."

These general qualifications are not all that special; they can reasonably be expected of anyone who professes to be a follower of Jesus Christ.

I heard about a management seminar in the secular business world in which a debate was going on about the qualifications for managers. One gentleman, listening to all the qualifications being spelled out, took out a New Testament, turned to Titus 1 and 1 Timothy 3, and pointed out to the leader of the seminar that they were paying an awful lot of money to hear from him what they could have gotten for nothing from the Bible. The interesting thing about it is that in management today, when they are looking for people who can give leadership, they want those who have basically the qualifications spelled out here in this passage of Scripture. This does not mean that we take lightly these qualifications. What it does mean is that elders are people whose lives show the characteristics of spiritual maturity that can reasonably be expected of those who are serious about the Lord.

Moral integrity

First, "An elder must be blameless." The word *blameless* here means a man whose life is characterized by moral integrity. In other words, he is firmly committed to Christian, biblical morality. And he is known to be firmly committed to this not only by the stands he takes but by the lifestyle he exhibits.

The apostle Paul, in the parallel passage, points out that this blamelessness has to be something that is not only recognized by believers, but is recognized and appreciated by nonbelievers too.

"He must also have a good reputation with outsiders" (1 Tim. 3:7). In other words, a person who is going to be suitable for this kind of leadership in the Christian church is a person who is known, both in the fellowship and in the secular world, as a person who clearly exhibits what biblical, spiritual, Christian morality is all about. And it would be utterly unthinkable for anybody to feel that they can be a leader of the church of Jesus Christ, of God's very own people, and not have that kind of lifestyle.

Sexual purity

Second, this elder is to be "the husband of but one wife." The Greeks have one word for both "man" and "husband." And they have one word that could be translated either "wife" or "woman." The word that is translated "husband" here is translated "husband" 50 times in the New Testament, but is translated "man" 156 times. By the same token, the word that is translated "wife" here is translated "wife" 92 times, but 129 times as "woman." Therefore, I think a very good case could be made for this expression literally to mean the elder has to be a one-woman man.

There's a rather colloquial twist to that, but it seems to me what the apostle is saying is that this elder has to be a man who is known for his sexual purity.

Sexual purity was particularly important in the early church. Because they were having so many problems with sexual immorality, it was absolutely imperative that they put some distance between the church and a corrupt and depraved society, particularly in the area of sexuality. I believe this emphasis is very necessary today. The church of Jesus Christ has to put a lot of distance between ourselves and the sexual immorality and impurity that has become normative in our society.

Therefore, my suggestion is that this expression, "The husband of but one wife," would probably be better translated "a one-woman man." However, if you want to leave it "The husband of but one wife," then you have to ask, how does this apply?

Some suggest that Paul was prohibiting anyone who was engaging in polygamy from being a leader in the Christian church. But Christian scholars say that is hardly the point, because if they were actually engaging in polygamy, they would not be allowed to function in any capacity in the church in the first place.

Others see in this statement a reference to divorce and remarriage. And some, including the church father Tertullian, have gone so far as to say that it could only be a man who had married once, and if his wife had died, he was not to remarry, or his eldership would be taken away.

If the expression is taken purely at face value, it would disqualify single men from eldership. That would mean neither the Lord himself nor Paul could have been elders!

Home Life

Paul goes on to say that this elder must be "a man whose children believe and are not open to the charge of being wild and disobedient." In the parallel passage in 1 Timothy, Paul explains why he believes this. And he adds what seems to be an incontrovertible rhetorical question: If a man can't manage his family, how on earth can he manage the church? This, of course, is a good question.

But what happens when you have an elder whose family is grown and gone? They are no longer his responsibility; he has little impact upon their lives. What about the person who has brought up his kids in a family where he was clearly a spiritual authority and recognized as the head of the family, where he gave his children every opportunity to grow up in the nurture and admonition of the Lord, and to all intents and purposes while they were at home they went along as consistent young believers, then they went wild after they left home? Is that person to be disqualified? That's something that must be carefully addressed.

It seems to me that we have to decide how long a father is responsible for his kids. I think one thing ought to be quite clear, and here we'll go to an irreducible minimum again: When we're talking about people who are qualified for eldership, we're talking about people who clearly are exercising spiritual leadership in their families. They are exhibiting leadership that is being accepted by the children. Furthermore, I think we're looking for people who have such a testimony in their family, where it's hardest to have a testimony, that their kids are being won over by the testimony of the old bearded one, the head of the family.

There is no guarantee that our children are going to believe. But if the father is running that family with no sense of leadership and in such a way that it is a disaster, if he is not demonstrating a winsomeness of spiritual experience, and the net result is that the kids are a mess, then it ought to be rather obvious that this person is not going to be qualified for eldership in the church of Jesus Christ. This is a serious thing, but I think the apostle Paul is making an awful lot of sense here. If I cannot exhibit in my own family leadership, authority, and winsome Christian testimony, and if I can't have an impact on my own kids, then it is highly unlikely that I could ever be able to have any meaningful leadership, exercise any spiritual authority, or make any powerful impact in the church of Jesus Christ.

The right personality

Since an overseer is entrusted with God's work, he must have what I call *personality suitability*. What Paul is saying about this is, there are some people whose lives just aren't under control. They are domineering people—violent in outlook and attitude, sometimes physically violent, but more often verbally violent. They are people who get into situations and stir them up. They are not disciplined as far as wine is concerned, and they are not disciplined as far as their own finances are concerned.

In other words, some of us have to recognize that there are personality quirks that indicate that we do not really have control of our lives. And if we don't have control of our lives, then we are not really suited for this kind of leadership. Let me hasten to add at this point that all of us have personality quirks and aberrations, and this is not saying that an elder is a person who does not have *any* quirks. I believe Scripture is saying that when a person's personality quirks, deficiencies, and inadequacies mean he is given to swings of mood, irrational behavior, and less than adequate control, that person would not be suited for eldership at this time.

Spiritual quality

Then Paul talks about *spiritual quality*. He says in verse 8 that the elder "must be hospitable." The Greek word for "hospitable" means, literally, "love strangers." That means he is a warm, openhearted person whose home is open to people. This was of crucial importance in the early church.

When evangelism took place in the early church, there weren't motels for the evangelists to stay in, and if there had been, they couldn't have afforded them. There were inns, but they were not suitable; therefore, the hospitality of people was a key factor in evangelism. If people weren't opening up their homes to these traveling evangelists, the evangelists couldn't go and preach. Moreover, there were many people who, when they became believers, upon being baptized were ostracized from their families. They had to go somewhere else to live. So hospitality was not only crucial for evangelism, but absolutely necessary for the caring and nurturing of new believers.

Hospitality is important today, if not quite to that extent. Somebody who is going to exercise an eldership function in the church of Jesus Christ has to be a person who is open-armed, openhearted, and open-homed, because he "loves what is good." This phrase is just one word in the Greek language, and it can mean a lover of good things or a lover of good people. In other words, this person has a genuine concern about that which is good, and he has a deep interest in people who are seeking, before God, to be good. If there's a good thing going, he wants to be part of it. If there's a good man around, he wants to identify with him. If there's something good that is happening, he's part of it.

But then Paul goes on to say that the elder is also "self-controlled, upright, holy and disciplined." In other words, this man has to be able to exhibit spiritual quality in these areas.

Sound doctrine

According to verse 9, this elder "must hold firmly to the trustworthy message as it has been taught." This person who is going to oversee, look after, and care for the church of God has to be a person who has been around long enough and has been interested deeply enough to really grasp the truth of the Christian gospel. In other words, he's got a good handle on theology and is deeply committed to the truth. Because of that, he is able to stand firm amid all kinds of spiritual and doctrinal confusion.

In the early days of the Christian church, when there was a considerable amount of spiritual and doctrinal confusion, it's rather obvious that the leadership had to be able to live above that confusion, to have their feet firmly set on the truth. I want to suggest to you that we're back in that position today. Any church can reasonably expect its leadership to be based in the truth, so that while confusion rages around and all kinds of different and crazy ideas are being propagated, the people can look to their leadership and see people who are staunchly stable themselves.

Understanding of the Word

Finally, an elder should also be able to "encourage others by sound doctrine and refute those who oppose it." The Word of God should have taken root in his own heart, but at the same time, he should be able to handle the Word of God so that when somebody needs encouragement or needs to be rebuked or some error needs to be refuted, he can minister the Word to that particular person or situation. That's the kind of person Paul is talking about.

Specific Qualities

Love for God's church

In verse 7, the apostle Paul says, "An overseer is entrusted with God's work." The word there is *overseer* or *steward*, meaning one who manages the affairs of another. I believe that one of the great things we need in a leader is a tremendous sense of privilege. An elder should constantly be asking, "Who am I, Lord, that you should have made me a steward of your very own people?"

Some people get into leadership in the Christian church and grumble and gripe about it all the time. They have no place there. To be in leadership, to be given the task of being a steward of God's very own people, is an inestimable privilege. And if we don't regard it as such, we shouldn't be there.

Love for God's Word

Second, if this leader doesn't love and study God's Word, he won't be deeply grounded in it himself and will not be able to minister God's Word to others.

I remember an occasion when I was preaching in another church, when I was called in front of the deacons (they were deacons, not elders, in that church) and was roundly rebuked for the way I had conducted the service that morning. What upset them was that I didn't give an invitation at the end of the service. I told them I would be happy to talk with them about it, and if they would open their Bibles, we would do a Bible study on invitations.

Well, it didn't take long to do a Bible study on invitations because none of them had their Bibles. So I said, "We've dealt with the problem you have. Let's do a Bible study on deacons. Who can tell me where deacons are mentioned in the Bible?" Not one of them knew one reference to *deacon* in the Bible. They were businessmen; they were traditionalists; they were men who had their own prejudices; but they were biblically illiterate men.

27

Such people have no place in a position of leadership. I believe an elder should be a steward who loves God's church, a student who loves God's Word, and a shepherd who loves God's people.

Love for God's people

We have already seen that the idea of overseeing and caring for is an integral part of eldership, and the specific expression *shepherding* is used quite a few times in Scripture concerning leadership. Paul, in Acts 20:28, speaking to the Ephesian elders, tells them that they are to shepherd God's flock. And you remember when the Lord Jesus gave instructions to Peter (who subsequently called himself an elder) to "feed my sheep" . . . "feed my lambs" . . . "shepherd my sheep." So an elder should be one who loves God's people and will give of himself to shepherd them; one who loves God's Word and will give of himself to study it; and one who loves God's church and will give of himself to manage, administer, and genuinely lead it.

Choosing the Elders

You will notice, first of all, that elders were appointed by the apostles. The Lord Jesus appointed his apostles, and they became the foundation of the church. But then, as the church began to move out of the apostolic era, it was obvious that the apostles would soon be gone. The elders, therefore, would be the next leaders. So the first elders were appointed by the apostles. In the book of Acts we see that Paul and Barnabas revisited churches and appointed elders. But you'll notice a slightly different development in Titus. Here we have an apostolic delegate who appoints elders. The point is that, in the Bible, the only way you ever hear of an elder being ordained is by appointment. The elders were appointed initially by the apostles, subsequently by apostolic delegates.

The second thing we need to note is that elders function in the local church *in the plural*. Some segments of the historic church have developed what theologians call *a monarchical episcopate*.

That means they have a bishop or an archbishop. This system was apparently developed in early church history after the apostolic era, but I believe it has no biblical foundation. Elders in Scripture are spoken of in the plural.

We need to note, third, that no appointment procedure is specifically stipulated in Scripture. And, fourth, there is no mention of a time limit of the elders' function. But we do need to bear in mind that Paul, speaking to the Ephesians, says that it was the Holy Spirit who had appointed them to be elders (Acts 20:28).

So however a church decides to go about appointing elders, they had better make absolutely certain that they are people who are called by the Holy Spirit for that ministry.

The Tasks of Elders

A church must be well fed

First, elders are to pay careful attention to doctrinal purity in the teaching and in the ministering of the church. Also, the elder is to ensure an abundance of teaching and counsel for the fellowship.

A church must be well led

Second, the elders are to have a clear sense of direction for the church. They are themselves to be leaders, but Peter tells us they are to lead primarily by example. They are to be clear-thinking people. Through vision and concern they are to think things through, develop a sense of direction, and by their very lifestyles encourage people to move in that direction.

If the church is to be well led, the leadership must encourage a "followership" attitude. The thing that determines whether or not you are a leader is if anybody is following. Therefore, elders have to generate in the fellowship an attitude of followership. If they can't do it, they're not leading. That means that there have to be the best possible relations between the elders and those they are caring for.

How you develop followership and how you maintain it needs careful examination. If there is ever an erosion of goodwill between the fellowship and the leadership you may as well put up the shutters, because all you're going to do is get yourself into continual fights and arguments, and that must not be. Not only must there be a tremendous sense of seriousness and privilege on the part of the elders, but on the part of the fellowship there has to be an attitude of willingness to acknowledge their leadership and follow their direction.

Paul, in 1 Thessalonians 5:12-13, says, "Now we ask you, brothers, to respect those who work hard among you, who are over you in the Lord and who admonish you. Hold them in the highest regard in love because of their work. Live in peace with each other." And Hebrews 13:17 exhorts us to "obey your leaders and submit to their authority. They keep watch over you as men who must give an account. Obey them so that their work will be a joy, not a burden, for that would be of no advantage to you."

A church must be well bred

Finally, we have to protect the church from any heretical influence and preserve it from any moral disintegration. And that means that discipline has to be exercised. In our church constitution we have a statement to the effect that people can be removed from membership if their doctrinal stance is no longer compatible with the church's position, or if their lifestyle is such that it is not compatible with what we stand for.

The people who are given the responsibility to lead, oversee, and care for the church ought to be able to smell a heretic a mile away. And they don't just turn a blind eye to him. They deal with him and pray at the same time. They recognize the necessity for caring both for the church and for the individual. And if the church is being dragged into the gutter by the immoral behavior of someone in that church, the elders have to deal with it.

One of the greatest needs in the contemporary church is leadership that willingly bears the burden, genuinely loves the church, wholeheartedly serves the Lord, and constantly encourages the people. Blessed indeed is the church where such leaders are found.

Making It Real

1. List the six *general* qualifications for elders in the church. Which of these can be reasonably expected of anyone who professes to be a follower of Jesus Christ?

2. What qualifications do we often look for in choosing elders today? How do these compare with the three specific qualifications noted in this chapter?

3. How can we tell whether a church is well led?

4. If you are a leader in your church, how do you measure up to the standards laid out in this chapter? If you are a follower, how can you help your leaders do their job better?

3
Protecting God's People
Titus 1:9-16

*T*he apostle Paul has told Titus, one of his young associates, to stay on in Crete. Individuals had come to Christ, and now they were being encouraged to form themselves into communities of believers called churches. The main task Titus has been given is to put things in order in those churches, including the appointing of elders to oversee and to care for the well-being of the church.

However, there is a much deeper, greater, and grander thing going on while Titus is humanly bringing together the details of these fellowships: God himself is in Crete at that particular time, purifying for himself a people who are his very own, eager to do what is good.

The theme of Titus is that, on the human level, these elders are responsible for bringing into order the life and affairs of the local church. But on the other level, while they are doing that, God is at work producing in that church a people who are going to be clearly identifiable, clearly distinguishable, utterly distinctive as a very special people, uniquely God's people in that area.

Whenever, therefore, we talk about the church, we may talk about organizational structure, institutionalized factors, church government, constitution, or whatever else may be necessary, but we must always remember that at the end of all things must be the purifying of a people for God himself, God's very own people.

With this in mind, I want to show you the importance of protecting God's people.

The letter Paul is writing to Titus at this particular time uses pretty tough language. He quotes a very uncomplimentary comment one of the Cretans made about people living in Crete. Then he says that the poet is absolutely right! Paul's concern, of course, is that along with all the infant churches being founded in different parts of the Middle East, these people in Crete are struggling; they have much opposition. There are many difficulties, not only in opposition to them as individual believers, but also in founding the churches. These new Christians are having a difficult time coming together and seeing themselves as God's very own people.

The apostle Paul says that one of the great responsibilities of the leadership of those churches is, among other things, to protect God's people and the fellowship of believers so they might be God's very own people.

The Sound Doctrine of the Apostles

In verse 9, Paul says that the responsibility of the elders, among many other things, is that they "encourage others by sound doctrine and refute those who oppose it." Paul says that the leadership of the church must be deeply committed to sound doctrine, making it constantly and abundantly available to the people for two reasons: first, for the nurturing and the encouraging of those who are believers; second, for the refuting of those who are in opposition.

Now he moves into an elaboration of what he means concerning the refuting of those who oppose individual believers and the establishing of local churches. The emphasis is still on sound doctrine. You'll find the expression recurring frequently in the Pastoral Epistles—the two Epistles to Timothy and this Epistle to Titus.

Sound doctrine is revealed

Paul is insistent that the sound doctrine delivered to him and to the other apostles is not manmade. He says quite categorically in

Galatians 1:11-12, "I want you to know, brothers, that the gospel I preached is not something that man made up. I did not receive it from any man, nor was I taught it; rather, I received it by revelation from Jesus Christ."

The church of Jesus Christ must constantly be reminded that fundamental to church life is the sound doctrine, the gospel of our Lord Jesus Christ, that was not made up by man, but was revealed by God.

It is a God-given revelation. This is what sets the church apart from the rest of society and is the fundamental difference between a Christian and a non-Christian. Society does not operate on the basis of God's revelations, but on the basis of human speculation. A Christian is tuned in to sound doctrine, to divine revelation. A non-Christian couldn't care less about it. He does whatever he feels he should do, or whatever his society allows him to do. Therefore, one of the fundamental distinctives of the individual Christian and the church is the high regard in which sound doctrine is held, because it comes from divine revelation.

Sound doctrine is relayed

The apostle goes on to point out that sound doctrine is not only revealed by God, but it must be relayed by those to whom it was being revealed. He has not spoken that which he thought of himself, but he has delivered—and here is one of his favorite expressions—what he first received. "For what I received I passed on to you as of first importance" (1 Cor. 15:3). He also introduced his teaching on the Communion service in that way (see 1 Cor. 11:23).

Sound doctrine is received.

Earlier in 1 Corinthians 15, Paul says, "Now, brothers, I want to remind you of the gospel I preached to you, which you received and on which you have taken your stand. By this gospel you are saved, if you hold firmly to the word I preached to you. Otherwise, you have believed in vain." Do you see the picture? Sound doctrine is revealed; sound doctrine is relayed; sound doctrine is received. It is received by those who hear; they believe and—the apostle puts it very graphically—they take their stand upon it.

What then is the basis of the individual Christian life? What then is the basis of the community of believers in the church? It is the basis of sound doctrine.

Sound doctrine is reflected

Look at the word *sound* that Paul uses in Titus 1:9. In the Greek it is the word from which we get our English word *hygiene* or *hygienic*. It literally means "sound" or "healthy" or "well." In fact, on occasions it was used as a greeting in the Middle East during the time of the apostle Paul.

I was rather pleased to learn this because years ago, in England, we had two American students in our Bible School. They were engaged, and they used to greet each other rather warmly every morning, much to the delight of the other students. He was called Gene (rather strange to English ears since it is a woman's name in England); she was called Ena. And their greeting always went like this: "Hi, Gene." "Hi, Ena." We could never quite understand what hygiene and hyenas had to do with each other.

But I discovered that their greeting was valid. Hygiene, which is also the Greek word here, is a greeting.

The point of it is, however, that when the apostle says that sound doctrine is the key, what he is really saying is this: The preaching that is being revealed, relayed, and received must be reflected, because sound doctrine is healthy and always health-giving. So if you want to find a healthy Christian, look for a Christian who is plugged into healthy teaching. If you want to find a healthy church, look for a church that is built upon healthy teaching. Both sound teaching and healthy doctrine produce health-giving living. When sound doctrine is imparted to individuals and to corporate groups of people, there will be evidence of vitality, health, and spiritual virility.

Why is it that individual Christians sometimes seem to be spiritually anemic? The answer quite simply is that they are deficient in sound, healthy teaching. Why do some churches seem to be withering on the vine? More often than not, it's because inadequate attention is being given to sound, health-giving, health-promoting teaching.

The apostle Paul, therefore, insists that the responsibility of Titus and the elders he appoints is to safeguard the propagation of healthy and health-giving teaching. If you're going to have healthy saints, you need sound doctrine. If you're going to have a healthy church, you've got to have sound doctrine.

It might be appropriate at this juncture to draw attention to another favorite Pauline expression: "This is a faithful saying!" A study of the many passages containing this phrase can prove most beneficial in identifying what Paul classified as "sound doctrine."

The False Teaching of the "Contradictors"

In total contrast to the sound doctrine and teaching of the apostles, Paul tells Titus that there is an awful lot of spurious teaching coming from the opposers, or more literally, the contradictors. *Contradict* means "to speak against," and the Greek word used here is the exact parallel. In other words, in and surrounding the community of believers there were those who were flatly contradicting sound teaching. They were opposers, contradictors, speakers against. And what they were producing was utterly spurious.

The apostle talks to Titus about it and says, "Your responsibility, Titus, and the responsibility of those elders who will be appointed, is to make sure you handle these spurious teachers and their spurious teaching correctly."

The contentiousness of the spurious teachers

The reaction of these spurious teachers to the gospel the apostle Paul and Titus had taught to Crete was utter rejection. They are described at the end of verse 14 as "those who reject the truth."

Now, let's face it. Whenever you present the gospel to someone, that person has the freedom to accept or reject what is being said. We are not responsible for people's response to or reaction against sound teaching. But we are responsible to see that they have the sound teaching, so they can either respond to it or reject it.

Always remember that in the propagation of the truth that was revealed by the Lord to his apostles and through them to the church, there will always be rejectors. There will always be those who don't want to do it God's way. But here's the ironic thing: That does not necessarily mean they want to divorce themselves from God's people. In fact, frequently you'll find that those who are resistant to what God says want to derive considerable benefit from God's people. And those who are living in blatant rejection of the truth still insist they have as much right to be God's people as those who accept the truth. But although those kinds of people in the community of believers have total freedom to reject the truth communicated to them, they do not have total freedom to go on propagating their rejection within the church.

The apostle not only outlines their reaction; he actually says that the sum total of their activities is rebellion. Their reaction is rejection; their activities can be characterized as rebellious activities. Verse 10 says that they are "rebellious people, mere talkers," deceiving all kinds of people. He says that you will find in and surrounding the Christian community those who reject the truth. But, for reasons known only to themselves, they still stick around God's people. They are rebellious in their lifestyle; they reject the truth committed to them; they do an awful lot of talking; and they are forever propagating what they believe. The end product is that they are deceiving all kinds of people and leading them astray.

"Titus," says Paul, "watch them. Don't allow these people to go around spreading their ideas; don't allow them to go around infecting God's very own people. See them for what they are. They are truth rejectors, and they are fundamentally rebellious against God."

He also has something very strong to say about their motives. He says that underlying all their activity is "dishonest gain." Financial considerations are underneath all they are doing.

Let's broaden that just a little and suggest that it is not uncommon to find people who reject the truth and are rebellious in their lifestyle, yet still demand and insist on having a place among the community of believers. They go on propagating their rebellion, insisting on their rejection, confusing and deceiving all kinds of people because they're getting benefit out of it for themselves. Not necessarily financial gain, but maybe they're getting a hearing. Maybe they're getting some attention. Maybe Christians are the only people who listen to them. Maybe it's the only chance they have of getting a crowd of people to even show any interest in them whatsoever. And Paul says to Titus, "Therefore, rebuke them sharply" (v. 13). Make sure their positions are refuted.

There is a feeling in society at large, and in the Christian community in particular, that if you refute anybody, you're cutting them down; you're rejecting them. All too frequently this is characterized as non-Christian. But if you allow those who reject the gospel of Christ to go on propagating their rejection, flaunting their rebellion, confusing and deceiving God's people, you're acting non-Christianly if you let them get away with it. It is not unchristian to sharply rebuke those who are in error; far from it. It is non-Christian to simply shrug your shoulders and assume it will go away or it doesn't matter or, even worse, to adopt the attitude of the pseudo-benevolent pastor who proclaims, "Well, everybody's entitled to his own opinion."

Everybody is not entitled to propagate spurious opinions in the community of believers. And it's the responsibility of the leadership to know what is being said by whom and whether there is spurious preaching. It is the responsibility of the leadership to rebuke it. Sharply.

The content of the spurious teaching

What were these people in Crete saying that was so wrong, that Paul was so concerned about? We don't have a clear statement of what it was that was so wrong, but there are numerous clues in the letters to Timothy and this Epistle to Titus that enable us to come up with some educated guesses as to what the specific nature of this spurious teaching was.

We know this spurious teaching was fundamentally *influenced by secular thinking*. For instance, in 1 Timothy 4:3, speaking of these teachers, Paul said: "They forbid people to marry and order them to abstain from certain foods." His answer to that is, "God created [these things] to be received with thanksgiving by those who believe and who know the truth." There you have a major difference between what the spurious teachers were teaching and what the Word of God teaches.

The Word of God teaches that God has given us these things richly to enjoy, but these teachers were saying that there are certain things you must not touch or eat. The tendencies were toward the ascetic. Their approach was this: There is something fundamentally wrong with matter, there is something fundamentally evil about the body; therefore, we have to rigidly watch this body and be very careful how we handle material things. And you become spiritual, they would say, by rigid and determined denial and discipline of the physical body and its God-given desires and needs, thus allowing the liberation of your spirit to take place.

First Timothy 6:20 gives us another clue in this regard. "Timothy, guard what has been entrusted to your care. Turn away from godless chatter and the opposing ideas of what is falsely called knowledge." These people who had ascetic emphases were also people who claimed to have special knowledge. The Greek word for "knowledge" is *gnosis*. Those who began to develop these ideas became known as *Gnostics*.

Gnostics had an approach to life that was in diametric opposition to what the Scriptures teach. They believed that God and spiritual things were totally separate from the world and material things. They claimed that God and things spiritual are essentially good; but the world and things material are fundamentally evil. This is called dualism. They did not believe that things came from one common source and that God was the beginning of all things. They believed that there were two sources; one that was good and one that was evil.

They believed that to be able to handle evil things you had to be able to handle the material. But they also believed that you needed special insight—special *gnosis*, special experience, special knowledge. And they believed they had it. They believed furthermore that if you didn't belong to their group you didn't have it. So what was the result? They suffered from a superiority complex. These people, rigid in their beliefs, believed they had a special "in" on the truth that was carefully refined, and that they were in a category far beyond and above everybody else. They demonstrated their superiority by utterly scorning the moral principles that were being taught in the church of Jesus Christ. They said these moral principles were either from the cosmos (which was evil and designed to bring us into slavery to it) or they were simply manmade ideas.

To show their utter scorn, Gnostics refused to adhere to the moral principles of the Scriptures—sometimes for ascetic reasons; sometimes they were just plain licentious. And they acted openly; they did their own thing because they thought they had an "in" on the truth.

The Gnostics had a powerful influence on the church. And Paul said, "Their teaching will spread like gangrene." That's complimentary, isn't it? "Among them are Hymenaeus and Philetus, who have wandered away from the truth." Paul goes on to tell what the Gnostics were teaching: "They say that the resurrection has already taken place, and [accordingly] they destroy the faith of some" (2 Tim. 2:17-18).

To say the resurrection had already taken place meant the only resurrection that would ever be was when Christ rose again from the dead. Gnostics maintained that to believe Christians will have a part in the Resurrection is total error. To them, it was utterly abhorrent to think that the body, which they considered so evil, would ever be raised up.

In teaching this idea they were denying the great hope of the believer, which is that one day we will be raised with Christ and will share eternal glory with him. This Gnostic influence that was coming into the church was purely secular. It had nothing to do with biblical revelation. In fact, more often than not, it flew totally in the face of biblical revelation.

Yet Gnostics reserved the right to breeze into the church with their secular thoughts and their secular teaching and confuse all manner of people.

It's the easiest thing in the world for people to become totally secularized in their thinking. Then they bring their thinking into the community of believers, demonstrating their utter biblical illiteracy, but chattering on about secular concepts and ideas, trying to twist them into biblical or spiritual principles. The secular world does not take time to find out what God's Word says, but they bring all their secular thinking to bear on the affairs of the church and try to fit the church into the mold of basic secular thinking. When people do that, the apostle Paul says, "Rebuke them sharply."

The second thing we can note about the content of this spurious teaching is that it was *involved in syncretic manipulations*. They were not only bringing in Gnostic influences; they were bringing in all kinds of Jewish influences and uniquely Christian ideas as well. And they were trying to form a syncretism of all three.

For instance, they loved some aspects of what the Gnostics were teaching, but they were really quite excited about many of the Jewish traditions, particularly what the apostle Paul calls all kinds of myths and endless genealogies and controversies (see 1 Tim. 1:4; Titus 3:9). These ideas fit in nicely with the way they were going. They even found some aspects of apostolic Christian teaching very interesting as well. So they pulled the whole bunch together and tried to make it all fit, then taught it in the church.

There is a great move in our society today to be delightfully and totally tolerant of what everybody believes and thinks. Often this is a commendable attitude, but very often we finish up with our tolerance producing total chaos. Particularly in the community of believers we try to bring in totally incompatible ideas, mold them together, and come up with a wonderful solution.

Let me give you one simple illustration. Do you remember TM, transcendental meditation? Do you remember how that was the big fad and how all kinds of believers got excited about it? They knew they were supposed to meditate, so they brought in Christian concepts of meditation and quoted things like "Wait upon the Lord."

Believers didn't like it, however, when it was pointed out that transcendental meditation is nothing more than Hinduism, dressed up to confuse people. They refuted it, rejected it, and detested it when they were told; but it was true nevertheless. And you would find, not infrequently, believers who were into TM. They said it really helped their spiritual growth. How Hinduism can help a Christian grow beats me, because it is a principle in total opposition to all that Christianity stands for. But this is the kind of thing that still goes on in the Christian church—syncretic manipulations.

So, in Crete, teaching was based on secular thought, with a syncretic amalgam of Jewish, Greek, and uniquely Christian ideas. They were going to be very tolerant, accept it all, and finish up with a delightful mishmash. This may sound great, but it is an utter insult to the basic principle that our truth is what God has revealed through the apostles and has preserved for us in his Word.

Third, these false teachers were *interested in all kinds of speculative fancies.* Paul points out in Titus 1:14 that they were all excited about Jewish myths. And in 1 Timothy 1:4, he talks about these same "myths and endless genealogies."

Some of the Jewish teachers felt there were gaps in the information made available to them in Scripture. So they set to work with great gusto and ingenuity, filling in these gaps with the most dramatic and fantastic details. The result was the most unbelievable speculative fancies imaginable. Today it is not uncommon for people to bring into the Christian community things that have the most tenuous relation to biblical truth; they are perhaps one percent biblical truth and 99 percent unbelievably fanciful speculation.

It's the easiest thing in the world for something like that to happen. Paul tells Titus to watch these guys, because if he's not careful he'll have a church full of people who are off into the most crazy, faddish, speculative hunches imaginable, assuming it to be good, sound, solid Christianity.

Then Paul also points out that their teaching *included much sensual behavior.* In Titus 1:16 Paul said that the people who are engaging in this kind of teaching "claim to know God." That is probably another passing reference to the *gnosis* idea. "They claim to know God, but by their actions they deny him. They are detestable, disobedient and unfit for doing anything good."

In case you need a commentary as to what Paul means specifically, read 2 Timothy 3:1-5: "There will be terrible times in the last days. People will be lovers of themselves, lovers of money, boastful, proud, abusive, disobedient to their parents, ungrateful, unholy, without love, unforgiving, slanderous, without self-control, brutal, not lovers of the good, treacherous, rash, conceited, lovers of pleasure rather than lovers of God—having a form of godliness but denying its power." Having a form of godliness, or as he says in Titus, "They claim to know God." But, by what they do, they deny that very claim.

Then see what he says—and please, ladies, I didn't say this, Paul did. "They are the kind who worm their way into homes and gain control over weak-willed women, who are loaded down with sins and are swayed by all kinds of evil desires, always learning but never able to acknowledge the truth" (2 Tim. 3:6-7). Now Paul isn't saying that all women are weak-willed. What he is saying is that some of them are; they're just like men in that regard. Weak-willed women are very susceptible to people who, in the name of spirituality, are actually engaging in all manner of sensuality.

Let's face it. Women who have been hurt, who are very lonely, who are having a hard time and are looking for some affection, are easy pickings for these kinds of people. Not infrequently, in our singles ministry, when individuals made loud protestations of spirituality it became abundantly clear to us that all they were interested in was rank sensuality, and some of the Bible study was taking place in bed. "Rebuke them sharply," says the apostle.

Let's take it a bit further. It is not uncommon in today's churches to find people who carry big Bibles; alongside the big Bibles and the Bible studies is a lifestyle characterized by rank sensuality and utter sexual immorality. "Rebuke them sharply," says the apostle.

The Consequences of Spurious Teaching

Paul's concern about this spurious teaching is that people's faith was destroyed. In another place he says they "shipwrecked their faith" (1 Tim. 1:19). Whole households have been turned upside down. In all this, people are falling into the trap of the devil and are being taken captive by him to do his will. In other words, the church of Jesus Christ had better recognize that alongside sound doctrine and holy teaching, there is always the possibility that some people, who identify with God's people, are propagating their totally nonbiblical views with endless chatter.

The net result of this will be that their teaching, chattering, and lifestyles will destroy the faith of some, make utter shipwreck of the faith of others, totally disrupt some households, and will result in some people being utterly captivated by the devil himself, so that they fall into unbelievable sin. And that's what Paul is warning Titus about. "You had better make sure you have some good leadership in that church, Titus, because this is the kind of junk that's going on. This is the kind of stuff that needs to be handled."

The Serious Responsibility of the Elders

Deal with the opposition

The serious responsibility of the elders in all of this is, first of all, to deal with the opposition—these people who are doing this damage.

First, *rebuke them sharply*. Everybody is going to say you're non-Christian; you're putting them down; you're cutting them off. Let them say it. Do what the Bible tells you to do. Rebuke them sharply.

Second, *silence them immediately*. As soon as you find out what they're doing, make absolutely certain that they are silenced immediately. And the word Paul uses for "silence" here means literally to put a muzzle on them. He says to the leadership of the church, get to this situation, rebuke these people, and take them out of positions where they have the opportunity of propagating what is in opposition to the Christian gospel.

If that sounds harsh, let me point out the third thing he says: *Teach them patiently.* Notice what he says in 2 Timothy 2:25. "The servant of the Lord must gently instruct, in the hope that God will grant them repentance leading them to a knowledge of the truth."

You have to rebuke them to point out the error of what they are saying. You have to silence them to protect those who are affected by what they are saying. But it doesn't mean you kick them out and say, "get out of here and get lost." By no means. Rebuke them, silence them, and then take every opportunity to patiently teach them, in hope that they might come to a knowledge of the truth.

Deal with the believers

Then there's a responsibility to protect believers from harm, to encourage them in growth, and to help them develop discernment.

I started out my working career as a banker when I was seventeen years of age, and nobody in the bank ever taught me how to recognize a counterfeit note. One day I said to one of the senior men, "Why doesn't somebody tell me how to recognize a counterfeit note?"

He said, "Oh, we never do that. We just give you lots of real ones to count. You'll get so used to counting the real ones that if you come across a counterfeit, you will know it."

I have no doubt that it is helpful for some people to study false teaching in order to recognize false teachers and false followers, but it is most important that we become deeply familiar with the truth. Not infrequently I have been surprised at the speed with which relatively new believers become aware of teaching that does not sound quite right. It's not because they have taken advanced courses in heresies, but because their hearts and minds are becoming attuned and accustomed to the truth in all its beauty. The more familiar they are with the real thing, the more readily they will identify the phony.

Making It Real

1. What is the primary thing, given in this chapter, that God's people need to be protected from?

2. Those who opposed sound doctrine in Paul and Titus's day showed rejection, rebellion, and reprehensible motives. How can we identify any opposers to sound doctrine today?

3. What kind of spurious teaching is around today? How does it compare with the spurious teaching of Paul's day?

4. How can we protect ourselves, corporately and personally, in the midst of the secularism, the pluralism, and the sensualism so rampant in our society?

4
Training God's People
Titus 2:1-10

*T*he apostle Paul, along with Titus, had ministered in Crete in an area that was totally ignorant of the truth. They had preached the gospel and invited the Cretans to come into a personal relationship with Jesus. Then Paul had to move on, but he left Titus there and said, "All right, now take them on from here, Titus."

It's one thing, of course, to lead people to a personal relationship with Christ. This is fundamental; this is basic; this is what we do in evangelism. But we are never given the mandate to leave them there. We are to disciple people in the arena of the fellowship of believers in the church of Jesus Christ. And so, Titus was given the task of going to each of the towns on Crete and organizing the believers, appointing elders who would oversee their spiritual life and ministry and well-being. In other words, establishing churches.

The church—on one hand an invisible, mystical, universal body, but on the other hand a local, tangible, visible body of believers—is actually God's very own people. And it is important not only that Christians individually know how to behave as those who have a personal relationship with Christ; it's very important that Christians collectively, as a body of believers, know how to behave, so they can model how people and communities are to be together.

So the apostle Paul gives Titus a monumental task—the task of appointing elders who will be able to lead, direct, oversee, encourage, and preach to a group of people so that they can be known as the people of God in that particular vicinity.

We have studied what the apostle told Titus in the first chapter of his Epistle, and we've noticed that the emphasis all along is on sound teaching, sound doctrine. That expression occurs also in the other two pastoral Epistles, Paul's letters to Timothy. It is obvious spiritual experience is based on the teaching of the Word of God, "healthy" teaching.

Paul emphasizes the necessity for healthy teaching because the pagan areas in which these people are living are infested with ideas, philosophies, and doctrines that are decidedly unhealthy. And so, in the midst of this unhealthy area, Titus is to insist on healthy teaching, truth from the heart of God, applied in such a way that it will produce healthy living in both individuals and the group as a whole.

Titus is also to be sure that the unhealthy teaching is being countered. God's very own people must be cared for by a proper overseer, who will teach them all that is correct. They have to be protected from things that would hinder, spoil, and mar their experience.

In the second chapter of Titus Paul gives some relatively minute details concerning the training of God's people. As we read through this passage of Scripture, we notice immediately that he divides the congregation into different groups. He talks about older men, older women; younger women, younger men; and disadvantaged people, like the slaves of that time.

The emphasis, as he divides this congregation into different groups, is on training them. That, of course, is the responsibility of those who have the oversight of a fellowship of believers. They must make the teaching available.

I often tell people in ministry, particularly when they get discouraged, "You can take a horse to water, but you can't make it drink." The responsibility of the elders, the leaders of the church, is not to make people drink. It is not to make them attend meetings. It is not to make them listen. It is not to make them feed. We can't do that. Many leave the ministry because they feel their responsibility is to make people do what it is patently obvious they are not interested in doing.

One of the greatest releases church leaders ever discover is that it is not their responsibility to make people learn. Their responsibility is to take the horses to the water, but not to feel they have to make them drink. But one thing I've learned is that they do have to make sure there's plenty of water available—plenty of teaching available—but an added incentive is that they should put plenty of salt in the oats. Keep the teaching available, so if there's any degree of life or interest in the people at all, they will want to be part of it.

So, if you find yourself basically interested in the opportunities for spiritual training, understand this: It is not the leaders' responsibility that you are interested. It is not their responsibility that you are doing nothing about it. Their responsibility is to make plenty of water available and put plenty of salt in your oats; and if you're not drinking after that, frankly, you've got a problem. If you have no appetite for sound teaching, no interest in discovering the things of God, then you are either spiritually dead or spiritually sick.

Having made the teaching available, it is then necessary for those who have been taught to know how to apply this teaching. And this is basically what Paul talks to Titus about in this passage.

The Intent of the Training

To explain what is sound

First of all, the intent of all spiritual training is to explain what is sound or healthy as opposed to unhealthy. Or, to put it another way, the intent of all spiritual teaching is to allow people to differentiate between that which is truth and that which is error.

There is considerable confusion in all societies now about what is true and what is false, about what is revelation of God and what is speculation of man. And the responsibility that rests upon those who oversee the church is to make sure people have every opportunity to understand the difference between sound and unsound, healthy and unhealthy teaching, and that they know the difference between what comes from God and what is manufactured by man. And that doesn't happen overnight. It's a long process. It is something to which we give ourselves constantly. And I would have to testify to you quite frankly that the more I personally study the Word of God, the more horrified I am at my ignorance of what it says.

I received a letter from England asking me to do the Bible teaching for sixteen thousand young people who would be gathering over there one summer. They asked me to teach a series of messages based on the prophet Isaiah. And the funny thing about it is that I had never, in over thirty-five years of preaching, preached a series on the prophet Isaiah. I thought, *Wow, if I take that on, I'm really going to have to work hard; I've been preaching thirty-five years and yet there are big holes in my knowledge of areas of the Word of God.*

I think we all need to be aware of the big holes in our knowledge of the Word of God and our understanding of the things of God. That is why it is so important that the teaching and training of the church of Jesus Christ be taken seriously so that we understand sound teaching. I am deeply alarmed at people who show little interest or involvement in sound teaching.

To emphasize what is suitable

I want you to notice an interesting little expression in Titus 2:1. "You," said the apostle to Titus, "must teach what is in accord with sound doctrine." The older versions of the Bible use a lovely old word: "That which is *becoming* sound doctrine."

What he is saying is, "You are to teach people that when they've got the doctrine straight in their heads, then they need to know what kind of behavior is becoming that sound teaching."

Let me give you an illustration. I've heard that there are some patterns and fabrics that are not very becoming to people who have certain body shapes. For example, some people should not wear fabrics with stripes that run in a particular direction or those stripes will accentuate what does not need accentuating at all. If you wear stripes that go the other way, they sort of help. I don't understand how it works; I'm not even sure if it's true. But the word that is used to describe wearing that which is suitable is *becoming*—"You are wearing a very becoming dress." "That hat is very becoming to you." It's an old English word, a nice word.

Paul's point to Titus is this: When you have taught the people sound teaching, train them to behave in a way that is becoming, that is suitable to the teaching you have taught them.

There is in all Christian teaching and training a direct link between Christian theology and ethics. There is a link between Christian profession and Christian performance, an application of Christian belief called "Christian behavior."

After people have had sound doctrine explained to them, they need to know what suitable behavior is. It is one thing to get the teaching right; it's another thing to get the behavior right. We must teach the truth. We must then help people understand that some kinds of behavior are just not suitable. Some kinds of behavior are, frankly, not in order as far as believers are concerned. And that tremendously powerful link between theology and ethics must be carefully taught.

We are all aware of this, but, unfortunately, it takes us time to understand and accept it. I could give you many illustrations of people who have come to Christ out of a basically pagan background; they really get into their Bibles; they understand Christian doctrine; they know the answers to a whole lot of questions. But, strangely, it takes a long time for the old pagan thought patterns to drop away and for the old pagan entanglements to be disentangled. We often find there's no difficulty at all getting people to study the Epistle to the Philippians, but it's hard getting them to bring behavior patterns into line with the principles they are learning.

That is all part of the church's responsibility. We are to emphasize what is suitable to those who understand sound teaching. And we must clearly show people what is improper. There are, after all, things that may be legitimate in a pagan society which, after you purposely and personally identify with Christ, become totally improper. And the new believer needs to make some changes.

To encourage what is strategic

There's another lovely little expression in verse 10 that I want to unearth for you, because it's not sitting on the surface. Talking about how slaves are to behave towards their masters, Paul said to teach them "not to steal from them, but to show that they can be fully trusted, so that in every way they will make the teaching about God our Savior attractive." Notice the emphasis on teaching again.

These slaves have been serving in their Christian community, living in their neighborhood groups, sitting in the Sunday morning service. They're really getting the teaching. The water's available, the oats are salty, and the slaves have been coming around and drinking.

But, said the apostle Paul, it is important that they also are trained to behave in such a way that their lives will make the teaching "attractive." The word used here is a very fascinating word—one that is used to explain what you do with a jewel to show it off to its best advantage.

If you watch the old Westerns, you'll remember the stories of the fellows who got the jewels and put them in a little bag they tied to their belts and stuck in their pockets. That really doesn't show off a jewel to its best advantage. What you have to do with a jewel is give it to somebody who can cut it right, then polish it, and put it in a proper setting. That is the Greek word Paul uses here. He says the responsibility of those who train the Christian fellowship is to get people who understand doctrine to so fit the doctrine into their lives that their lives become the proper setting for the jewel of truth. To me, that is a most delightful concept.

But think of it for a minute. All those people who say, "Don't bother me with doctrine; don't bother me with teaching; don't bother me with theology and all that kind of stuff" really don't understand that we need to be bothered with doctrine and teaching and theology—because people need to understand it. Let's face it. Most people aren't going to go to school to learn it. Most people don't want long sermons that teach it. Most people most definitely are satisfied with one dose a week. So they must have it presented to them in a different way. And the apostle Paul says that you present the reality of doctrine and theology in teaching by making sure that your life is a strategic presentation of it; a suitable setting for the jewel of truth. And that takes a lot of work, a lot of discipline, and a lot of help.

It is relatively easy to keep doctrine in the abstract and theology in an ivory tower. And a lot of us think that the real heavy stuff of the Word of God belongs in the seminaries or to the pastors. However, what the apostle is telling Titus is, "Go to those Cretans and teach them the truth about God, man, salvation, eternity, the truth; then get their lives into shape so that they become a setting for the jewel of truth so that it stops being abstract and becomes something very beautiful in the lives of the people."

Can you see what an enormous task rests upon the church of Jesus Christ? Can you see the responsibility of the leaders in the church? Their responsibility is to be explaining what is sound, then emphasizing what is suitable, and encouraging people to make their lives a strategic setting for the truth of God. And it doesn't happen overnight. It takes a lot of work, patience, teaching, and training. Yet that's what the church is supposed to be doing.

To engage what is skeptical

Explaining what the older women are supposed to be teaching the younger women, the apostle Paul says in verse 5 that, if the younger women do things properly, the results will be "that no one will malign the word of God."

There are a lot of people who are skeptical about the Word of God, skeptical about those people who claim to be Christians, born-again, or Spirit-filled, or whatever other adjectives we now find necessary. I think very often they have reason to be skeptical, because we make some big claims. We sit in our pews and sing quite happily that we are holy and blameless before the Lord.

Do you believe you're holy? Do you believe you're blameless before God? It is relatively easy for us to use holy clichés and ideas and propagate them without realizing that, when we make those statements, there are some people who wander in who may even be listening. They could say, "Those guys really think they are holy and blameless? They've got to be kidding." And they go away and laugh behind our backs. And our clichés and professions of faith become the means whereby they begin to rip Christ himself to shreds.

The apostle Paul said, "We have to get some training here so we take that opportunity away from them, so we can know that we are living among skeptical people who are going to level all kinds of criticism at us. As we live among the skeptics, our lives will be so in tune with our doctrine that they will really be hard put to genuinely criticize what we're doing."

Some people are greatly gifted when it comes to criticism. I sometimes wonder if the gift of criticism isn't the most common gift in the church of Jesus Christ. I certainly believe that sometimes it is the most ardently exercised gift. There's no question that everybody can find something to criticize in everybody else sooner or later. But we've got to realize that a lot of criticism is grossly unfounded and utterly unfair. A lot of criticism is more a reflection on the aberrations of the one doing the criticizing than on the person being criticized. Having said all that, our responsibility in training is to do things in such a way that we take away from them the opportunities for skepticism.

Then notice verses 6-8. Paul tells the young men they have to behave in a certain way, and Titus himself has to model what he is teaching them "so that those who oppose you may be ashamed because they have nothing bad to say about us." We are to teach people to bring their lives so in tune with their doctrine that the skeptics who live among us will be so frustrated that even though they would love to be able to utterly discredit us, they just can't do it.

There's a newspaper in North Carolina that, claiming to get at truth, apparently has spent decades looking for ways to discredit Billy Graham. The newspaper will periodically, regularly, even monotonously, go after him. The interesting thing about it is, though they have tried him at every point and have gone after everything they can, his reputation is still intact. No thanks to the newspaper.

There are plenty of people who will do all they can to besmirch a reputation and rip a character to shreds. The responsibility of those in the church of Jesus Christ is to know that we live among those kinds of people and that we are going to have to take what they give us. But let us teach and train people so that our detractors are hard put to find anything that is inconsistent. The responsibility of the church is to be training people, so that the doctrine they say they have received is being applied in their lives.

The Extent of the Training

Paul gives us some practical clues about the extent of the training.

Managing the people
The apostle divides the congregation into its natural groupings, which shows that he is actually managing the people well. He talks about those who are male and those who are female because men need one kind of emphasis and women need another. If you're going to teach men, you're going to teach them one way. If you're going to teach women, you're going to have to teach them another way. Paul obviously recognizes this, and he gives specific instructions on how to train the men and how to train the women.

He talks about the young and the old. Young people are going to go for one thing; old people are going to go for another. If we're going to train the young people, they're going to need one kind of emphasis; the old folks probably won't go for much at all, but we'll try what we can with them anyway. And he puts a different emphasis there.

Then, of course, there are those who are deprived or disadvantaged, and those who were born with a silver spoon in their mouth. They all have different problems, different interests, different prejudices. The have-nots are intent on having what the haves have, and the haves are intent on insuring that the have-nots have not what the haves have. That being the case, Paul says, "We have to recognize that we're going to have to teach the haves how to handle what they have and teach the have-nots how to handle what it means to have not what they have not, and begin to work in these areas."

So, the apostle Paul tells Titus, rightly manage the people by recognizing the different situations and then organizing the necessary education for them.

Mobilizing the team

I think when Titus got to Crete and received his instructions from Paul, he probably sent a cable right back and said, "Paul, when you said all the towns of Crete, is that what you meant? You mean you want me to do this in *all* the towns of Crete? How about *one* of those nice little towns in Crete? I've found myself a nice place here."

"No," Paul said. "I want you to establish churches in all the cities of Crete. I want you to ordain elders in all the cities of Crete."

Titus replied, "I can't do all that. How can I do all that? Only so many hours in the day, you know, Paul."

Paul said, "I know. I didn't tell you to do it yourself. I told you to see that it's done. Get the difference?" Notice the two things Paul immediately tells him.

First, Paul tells him to go and ordain elders in every place—elders who themselves are going to teach, train, equip. It was to be a team effort, a team ministry.

One of the greatest disasters in the church of Jesus Christ in recent years has been this utter fallacy that you pay a pro to do it all. That's why a lot of churches are small. They can't be anything other than small for the simple reason they have only one person doing it all, and the size of the church is determined by the extent of his energy. When he's out of energy, gas, and ideas, the church is out of growth.

On the other hand, when people are managing different ministries, then a team is being built so that the burden is being shared, the load is being disseminated, and authority and opportunity are being delegated, then you are not limited by one man's energy. This has always been the New Testament principle. We lost it for centuries when somebody dreamed up this clergy-and-laity dichotomy.

The Scriptures are quite clear that those who are elders, those who are pastor-teachers, those who are apostles or prophets, have the responsibility to equip people to do the work of the ministry—training. Are you in your church appointing elders and equipping leaders? Do you have pastor-teachers who are able to operate in such a way that the immense load of your fellowship is being realistically handled?

But Paul doesn't just talk about the elders. He talks about motivating the older women as well. He says that the older women are to be equipped "to be reverent in the way they live, not to be slanderers or addicted to much wine, but to teach what is good" (v. 3). In other words, the women have a special responsibility too. And uniquely in this environment and culture, he said they are to be equipped to train the younger women. The team is taking shape.

"I didn't tell you to do it all yourself, Titus. I didn't tell you to rush around all those cities in Crete and do it all yourself. Manage the people properly, then mobilize a team and motivate the people."

Modeling the truth

People don't just hear what we say. They watch what we do (which is rather unnerving). That's exactly what the apostle Paul says to Titus: "In everything set them an example by doing what is good. In your teaching show integrity, seriousness and soundness of speech that cannot be condemned" (vv. 7-8). In other words, teach them the truth and model it in your life.

My wife, Jill, was talking to Ray Stedman's wife one day about this whole business of people's expectations. She was talking about the pressure of trying to be a role model, knowing her own weaknesses and frailty, her own failures and fallenness, her own sinfulness—the stuff we all cope with. What Elaine Stedman said was very helpful, and we wanted to share it with you: "We're called to be models, Jill. But we're not called to be models of perfection. We're called to be models of growth."

Perfection is what people expect of you, and that's tough. Generally, they don't expect it of themselves; they expect it of other people. It's an unrealistic expectation.

But people can rightly expect that those in positions of leadership lead and model the truth in an increasingly mature and valid way. If we are in a position of teaching and training people, we must recognize that what we say will have some impact, but what we do and what we are is probably going to have a much greater impact. If we combine what we are saying with what we are doing and teaching and what we are, then the balance is going to be powerful indeed. The extent of the teaching requires the modeling of the truth from those who are doing it, a lifestyle that is consistent, and communication that shows real conviction.

One way you can show conviction in your communication is to give the impression that you know what you're talking about. And if you're trying to teach somebody something, give them the impression that you're prepared, that you've done your homework, that you're not just getting up and shooting from the hip. Far too much of that goes on.

I'm appalled at Sunday morning talks that are really Saturday night specials. Last-minute rehashes of the few things teachers know, the few things they've learned. You are going to communicate conviction about that truth if it is perfectly obvious that you have taken the time to figure out what it is and get it across to other people.

Maintaining the pressure

I'm just going to touch on verse 15 because I will cover it more in the next chapter. Paul says in summary, "These, then, are the things you should teach. Encourage and rebuke with all authority. Do not let anyone despise you."

Notice: In the church of Jesus Christ, those who are called to oversee, teach, train, equip, and lead are required to maintain pressure on the people who are members of the people of God by a proper application of the truth. Sometimes people need a word of encouragement. Make sure they get it. Other people need a word of rebuke. Make sure they get it. Other people need a sense of authority in those who are presenting truth. Make sure they accept that authority. Paul says, "Don't let anybody schlepp you off, Titus. You're my man there. You're going as a delegate of the apostolic truth."

I've often said to people that Stuart Briscoe, as one of the pastors of Elmbrook Church, has no intrinsic authority. But Stuart Briscoe, when he stands in the pulpit with God's Word, has authority, and you'd better believe it. It is not the authority of my person or my position. It is the authority of God's Word that I present.

If people need rebuking in the name of the Lord, based on the Word of God, we fail them if we don't rebuke them. On the other hand, if people need a word of encouragement and we're just pontificating, and there is no personal application, then we're failing them. And if people are simply walking away from a situation and saying, "Get off my back. What's that got to do with me?" and we as leaders let them get away with it, we're failing them. We are not to let people despise those who minister God's Word. We are not to let people simply shrug their shoulders and disregard those whom God has put in authority over his people. His people need leadership, and the leadership better know what it's doing. So those of us in any kind of leadership better maintain the right pressure.

The Content of the Training

Paul was aware that different people need to be taught different things, depending on their unique circumstances. Accordingly, he instructed Titus to give careful attention to the older men, the older women, the younger women, the younger men, and the slaves (whom we will call the disadvantaged.) Each group was to be taught the things Paul thought they most needed to hear.

The older men

Our society puts a premium on youth and youthfulness. We are familiar with advertising that tries to convince us our gray hair can be turned back imperceptibly to its "natural color" (presumably because gray is unnatural), and pictures showing a couple of beauties in sleek swimsuits sporting identical wide grins full of sparkling teeth, billowing blonde hair, and sparkling blue eyes, only to be asked to decide which one is the mother of the other! As a result there is a subtle message that "young" is desirable and commendable and "old" is something considerably less. To the extent that Western society has lost sight of the mellow value of older age in the dazzling blaze of youth, our society has lost an asset of experience and maturity that is irreplaceable.

It is true that Ronald Reagan reversed the trend to some extent with his considerable youthful vigor, but not without the press reminding us that he dozes off in cabinet meetings and papal audiences and needs Nancy's help fielding questions when his hearing aid malfunctions.

Other societies regard older people considerably more highly, a natural progression from the veneration of ancestors. The people Paul was dealing with would, therefore, understand that older men should be respected, and this required them to behave with the dignity and maturity appropriate to their advancing years. They were to be "temperate, worthy of respect, self-controlled"—meaning that if they expected to be respected they would have to earn respect. This would require discipline on their part. Status and gray hair partially earns respect in some quarters, but inappropriate behavior by older people earns a disproportionate amount of approbation.

My mother had a particular distaste for older people who dressed and behaved younger than their years—"Mutton dressed up as a lamb!" she sniffed. Perhaps she had been unduly influenced by her mother, who repeatedly told all who would listen, "There's no fool like an old fool!"

The older men were also to ensure that their behavior had a clearly discernible spiritual quality. They were to be sound (healthy or robust) in their faith, their love, and their endurance. Older people should have a healthy working knowledge of the theological content of faith and demonstrate a trusting attitude and a faithful commitment.

Some older people tend to become increasingly self-centered in their later years, but Paul wanted Titus to remind them that they have a lot of love to give and that they should seek out those most in need of loving care and support. As they grow older, their powers begin to wane, and their influence begins to disappear, and they can easily become discouraged and defeated. But this must not happen; the older men have much to offer. They must not quit; they must not become self-absorbed; they must not become cranky and disgruntled. They must keep the faith and keep their cool and keep on keeping on.

The older women

Turning his attention to the older women, Paul wisely does not define the term *older*, but he is most forthright in his instructions, which fall into two categories. He tells Titus to warn them of weakness and to channel them to constructiveness.

Apparently the older women were spending their time in slanderous gossip and overindulgence in wine tasting. The former would be detrimental to good relationships, the latter, patently self-destructive. Gossip has been defined as "sharing something you like about somebody you don't" and, unfortunately, many of us, not just older women, are ill-disciplined in both hearing and speaking things that are best left unshared. Women who turn to drink, as many of our modern soap operas document daily, are usually desperately lonely women who have no significant involvement in life. They feel unwanted and useless, grovel in feelings of inferiority and irrelevance, and show their inner disgust and loathing by carefully calculated self-destructive behavior.

These women, in Paul's day, as in ours, need to be channeled into constructive behavior. They need to be taught "reverent" behavior, and they themselves should become teachers of what is good. The word translated "reverent," used only here in the New Testament, means "suitable to a sacred person, service, or circumstances" and could possibly refer to an order of older women, *presbutidas*, similar to the "older men"—or elders, *presbuteroi*. Whether or not these women were recognized as leaders in their churches, they were clearly admonished to invest their lives in profitable and honorable behavior.

The younger women

The ministry of the older women was to be particularly, but not necessarily exclusively, directed to the younger women. The word *younger* has connotations of "new" or "fresh" and may refer to those women who were "newly" married although not so "freshly" married that they did not have children! The instructions for these women are more numerous than those for any of the other groups. They are "to love their husbands and children" (v. 4), or literally to be "husband-lovers and children-lovers."

At first sight it might appear unnecessary to train people to do this, as we tend to assume that this kind of love is spontaneous and inevitable. But Paul and Titus, and all other people involved in marriage counseling, know that love in the family is more than a feeling. We all need help in learning how to show love in practical ways and how to love those whose love has grown cold and whose behavior is reprehensible.

How many people have needed help in dealing with wayward and rebellious children? How many brokenhearted young women have not known how to handle their anger and resentment against a drunken, abusive, unfaithful husband? Self-control is something that all age groups need to learn, and Paul mentions it in relation to both older and younger men as well as younger women.

Perhaps the young married woman with small children constantly demanding her attention, and a husband who may be less than sensitive to her needs, would be prone to irritability and might on occasion give vent to her feelings with a knock-down-drag-out confrontation or an ear-shattering screaming match. Training in how to cope would be most helpful in heading off such potentially catastrophic situations.

"Pure" would certainly include sexual propriety but was much more far-reaching in that it spoke of inner motivation in all areas of life. Young women may be tempted to engage in all kinds of questionable actions because they are limited in what they can do and say. Therefore, when they want to use subterfuge and deceptive manipulation to get their own way they must refrain. "Feminine wiles" and "pure" motivation are hardly compatible.

Most young wives and mothers know that running a household is a major undertaking. Therefore to tell them to be busy at home may seem to be an unnecessary admonition. However, there have always been younger women who have neglected home and children in the same way that there have always been older women who drank too much and talked too much. The problem for both would probably be traced to boredom and/or laziness. In some instances younger women have needed training because they never learned the practicalities of running a household. In our church we have found that the Young Moms ministry has been particularly helpful in providing experienced help and encouragement in this specific area.

Of course it is possible to be as busy as a bee and as unsociable as a hornet. Martha of Bethany, for example, while she was busy doing what she felt necessary, was becoming quite resentful about her busyness and irritated with all who got in her path. The answer to that is to teach a kind spirit. Perhaps this can be done best by elevating the value of running a home and family in the popular perception and being careful to express appreciation for all that the hard-working homemaker does. Perhaps husbands and children could encourage the young mothers by being helpful and appreciative themselves, at least occasionally!

The final instruction relates to husband-wife relations with particular reference to the wives being "subject to their husbands." While this instruction is the cause of much debate in our modern society, it would cause no debate in Paul's day for the simple reason that in first-century society women were given no other option than to be subject to their husbands, since they were regarded as little more than property and chattels. We need, therefore, to ask why Paul would make such a point of female submission and, in other places, male headship, seeing it was a foregone conclusion. The answer would appear to be that the unique emancipation that the Christian gospel had brought to women may well have led to an attitude among the women that was less than respectful to their menfolk and, accordingly, scandalous to the secular society. If Paul's instruction was mildly surprising to the women, his instruction that men should love their wives as Christ loved the church was revolutionary, and his teaching on men and women subjecting themselves to each other was positively mind-boggling!

Paul and Titus were well aware of the radical societal changes the gospel was introducing, and they recognized that too many changes too soon could cause a backlash effect, which, in turn, would give their opponents an opportunity to "malign the word of God." Rather than allow that to happen, God's people have always found it necessary to govern their behavior and even, at times, curtail their own legitimate freedoms for the sake of the gospel.

The younger men

Surprisingly, the younger men were to be taught only one thing, and that was to be "self-controlled." As we have seen, the same instruction was to be given to other people as well, but perhaps it was necessary to mention only self-control because if young men got a handle on that the rest would be relatively easy for them. Being men, of course, they had far more freedom than the women, who were secluded in their homes, discouraged from appearing in public, not allowed to work outside the home, and generally treated in a manner similar to that practiced by fundamentalist Muslims in their homes. The more freedom granted, the more self-control is needed.

Being young also necessitates self-control, and the two are not easy bedfellows! "Youthful exuberance," "high spirits," and "fun-loving" are all common terms, some euphemistic, that not infrequently describe irresponsible, destructive, and abusive behavior. Granted, much of it is unthinking and benign, but careful training helps even young people look before they leap, thus saving them from the malignant effects of benign youthful intentions.

The slaves—or the disadvantaged

If the gospel brought new status and opportunity to first-century women, young and old alike, it also introduced the seeds from which the full flower of the emancipation of slaves flourished. The Hebrews had always adhered to strict rules concerning the ownership and treatment of slaves, many aspects of which served not only to alleviate their suffering but also, in many instances, to rescue the unfortunate from penury and even starvation. The same could not always be said for the slaves of other cultures, and the gospel message, with its emphasis on God's concern for the humble and the poor and their exalted position in the eternal kingdom, came to them like a breath of sweet, fresh air after the dank odors of a fetid prison cell.

But in the same way that the younger women needed to be trained not to abuse new freedoms, the slaves needed to be taught how to behave as spiritually emancipated yet socially disenfranchised people. Their instructions all dealt with their relationships to their masters. They were to be "subject" to them, which, of course, was not new as the women's mandatory subjection to their men was not new. The slaves were placed in a position of enforced subjection and servitude. The difference, however, was that they would subject themselves voluntarily from the heart as opposed to the surly, uncooperative kind of subjection that is so common among those who are powerless. This would be shown in the genuine desire "to try to please" their masters.

Note that they are "to try to please," which is a very realistic instruction given the fact it is impossible to please some people. Evidently, slaves had become so truculent because of their under-privileged status that it was common for them to "talk back" to the masters and, whenever they had the chance, to "steal from them." It would, no doubt, be easy for them to rationalize such behavior both on the grounds that it was common practice and because it was the only way they could compensate for the abuse they were suffering.

Christian slaves, however, had a higher and nobler concern—they were to "make the teaching about God our Savior attractive." One way they would do this was by showing that they could be "fully trusted."

In many ways slavery has long since vanished from the scene, and the advent of the Christian gospel had much to do with its demise, but racial discrimination is still with us, abuse of the under-privileged is not uncommon, and the powerless are still dominated. And the gospel still applies in two ways. Those who serve a God of justice need to represent him to and on behalf of the disadvantaged, and the Christians among the disadvantaged need to be encouraged to live well in their circumstances until the slow moving wheels of change make life more pleasant and just for everyone. In so doing they cannot help but make the gospel attractive, because nothing calls attention to the message of grace quicker than gracious living under pressure.

Making It Real

1. How are the elders responsible for training God's people?

2. What are the four goals listed for the spiritual training of the people? How can the church accomplish these four goals?

3. What were the instructions given to each group of people: older men, older women, younger women, younger men, and slaves? How could following these instructions make the teaching about God attractive to the rest of the world?

4. Based on this chapter, what is one thing you would like to do to make it obvious that you are one of God's very own people?

5
Purifying God's People
Titus 2:11-15

*I*f you go to the Golden Gate in San Francisco, you will see a narrow inlet; it's two miles across and four miles long. On each side of the inlet, there are rather steep hills, and a deep channel comes through the strait. The strait opens up on one side to the Pacific Ocean and on the other side to San Francisco Bay. When people wanted to get from the San Francisco peninsula to northern California, and vice versa, they used to have to travel all the way around the bay. So somebody came up with a great idea. They decided they would try to bridge the gap. They built something we are all familiar with, something all the tourists want to see no matter where they come from: the famous Golden Gate Bridge.

Those of you who are familiar with the outline of the Golden Gate Bridge know that it is supported on only two towers. Fastened to these towers are massive cables, and from these massive cables are all kinds of other cables on which the bridge is suspended. That, strangely enough, is why they call it a suspension bridge.

In the same way, God has a lot of people standing on one side of a deep chasm, and he wants to get them to the other side. But he has a problem: how to bridge the gap. To rightly understand the ministry of Christ and the Christian church, we have to understand where people are, where God wants to take them, and the bridge he is going to use to get them there. That's what Paul talks about in Titus 2:11-15.

God's People Problem

Let's get hold of the real situation as we confront it, or, more importantly, as God confronts it today. Notice four things this passage of Scripture tells us about the situation mankind is in: In verse 12 we are told of ungodliness, worldly passions, and a mention of this present age. There are three terms that bear careful looking into—*ungodliness, worldly passions, present age.* They clearly describe the situation of humanity as God sees us on one side of the chasm that separates us from our Lord.

Ungodliness

Ungodliness means that we have an attitude and a lifestyle that clearly demonstrate we are not serious about God. The Greek word used here is the exact opposite of the word *godly* that occurs so often in the Pastoral Epistles. God wants people to be godly. The root idea of that word is "to take God seriously." The problem, God says, with our society and with our lives, is that we do not take him seriously and we exhibit this in the activities we find so attractive.

Worldly passions

Worldly passions is tied in with the expression *the present age,* and they are really two biblical terms for what we call today *secularism.* The word *secular* is related to the idea of the world, and it has to do with an attitude of heart and mind and a lifestyle that show we are more interested in the age in which we live than in the age to come. And we are fundamentally more attracted to a life that is rooted in the material things in this world than we are concerned about the spiritual things of the world to come.

This present age

Webster's Dictionary has a marvelous definition of secularism: Secularism is "a system of social ethics based upon a doctrine that ethical standards and conduct should be determined exclusively with reference to the present life and social well-being, without reference to religion."

In other words, there is a system of social ethics in our world based on the idea that all that really matters is social well-being now, in the age in which we're living, without any reference to religion at all. Secularism is an attitude of the mind that produces an ethic for individuals and society as a whole that carefully and calculatedly rules out eternity and absolute standards, and has nothing whatsoever to do with Christian ethics.

That is the situation in which we find our society today. There's nothing new about it; it has always been the case. Different societies at different times have been able to disguise this rather carefully and cleverly. But the interesting thing about the present time is that we are no longer bothering to disguise it. It is abundantly clear that the basic approach to life in our society is that there is an ethic that is determined exclusively with reference to the present life, the social well-being, without any reference whatsoever to God. And there is evidence of this on every hand.

I had a free evening not so long ago, which in itself was something of an experience for me. The telephone didn't ring; no one came by. I was so taken aback by this unusual situation that I sat down, switched on the television, and spent one of the most depressing, boring evenings of my life. I went to bed with a heavy burden on my heart for all the dear people in this country who have nothing better to do than to watch television.

Now, I'm not going to start a rampage against television. I like the news; I like the sports; and I like, quite frankly, PBS, because they show a lot of BBC programs. But the utter emptiness, the utter deadness of what was being presented was unbelievably depressing.

I was discussing my dismay with somebody who asked, "Have you watched the afternoon soaps lately?"

I said, "I haven't watched afternoon soaps in years."

She said, "Watch a few sometime. If anything, they're even worse."

What is our television doing? It is simply portraying our society. And we know perfectly well that because television operates on the profit motive, it is giving us exactly what we want. What does that say about our society? Nothing more than that we have become tremendously active in our ungodliness, we are deeply attracted to secularism, we are anchored in this present age.

Because we are so swamped with ungodly and wicked attitudes, because they are rooted in worldly passions in this present age, very often we don't even know how much we are governed by them. We don't even know how much our thinking, our ethics, and our activities are simply modeling that which is contrary to all that God is. That's God's people problem.

Bridging the Gap

What is God going to do about this situation? Getting back to our illustration of the Golden Gate Bridge, we can answer this question. Remember those two towers? As you read this passage of Scripture in Titus, you'll see standing out of it two great big towers. And they are identified by the word *appeared* or *appearing*. I want you to note this word very carefully. In verse 11, Paul says, "The grace of God that brings salvation has appeared." Then you'll notice in verse 13 he says, "While we wait for the blessed hope—the glorious appearing of our great God and Savior, Jesus Christ."

In one sense *epiphany*—or appearing—can be used to describe the sudden burst of light that happens at sunrise. I've often taken overnight flights around the world. And one of the greatest moments is when, instead of the dawn coming imperceptibly, the sun suddenly bursts over the horizon. That is an epiphany in the sense in which the Greeks used it; it means a sudden appearance.

But the idea was taken and used in many different ways. For instance, the Caesars of those days would use *epiphany* to describe a dramatic appearance of themselves in a certain situation. When Queen Elizabeth II toured the U.S. West Coast, it was interesting to see the response on the part of many people. They recognized something of majesty and awe, something indefinable about her. And when she appeared, the people gathered around and, with some exceptions of course, seemed to be pleased to see her. Now then, this was an appearance, an epiphany, a majestic appearance.

Two towers: the first and second coming of Christ

God has planned two majestic, dramatic appearances, and they are the towers of the bridge he is building. The first one is an historical epiphany; it has already happened. The second one is an eschatological epiphany; it is yet to happen.

The first tower is the epiphany of grace. *Grace* is a term with which we are familiar; we hear it quite often. What it really means is "God's unmerited favor which comes from his unsolicited choice." Mankind—ungodly, wrapped up in worldly passions, rooted in the present age, enjoying her wickedness, making excuses for it—is not particularly interested in getting to God and saying, "God, please intervene." God's intervention in the human condition far predates man's desire for anything different. The reason God intervened in the human condition is quite simply because he determined to give us, unsolicited and unmerited, what we didn't deserve. It was his free choice; it was his initiative; he decided to do it.

The epiphany of grace, this unmerited favor of God, was portrayed in the Incarnation. Our Lord Jesus laid aside his glory, assumed our humanity, and appeared on earth. For thirty years he was majestically, dramatically among us, demonstrating God in the flesh. At the end of those thirty-three years, he laid down his life. On the third day he rose again from the dead, showed himself openly, and in so doing, showed what God was prepared to give us for no other reason than that he chose to be gracious to us.

Incarnation, crucifixion, resurrection—these are the terms that come under the heading of the great tower of the epiphany of grace. What God has chosen to do about the human condition is built on that first tower. He has chosen to give us the Incarnation. He has chosen to give us the Crucifixion. He has chosen to give us the Resurrection. It is a ministry of grace.

But you can't suspend a bridge on one tower. There have to be two. Accordingly, there are two epiphanies. The second tower is the epiphany of glory. And Paul tells Titus that those who understand the grace of God and are thrilled by it and say, "God, how wonderful that you should deal with us in grace," are anticipating the other epiphany. They are people who, because of their excitement about what God has done in grace, are excited about what God is going to do to finalize all he has in mind.

What is he going to do? He has planned another dramatic epiphany, another appearance. In the same way that the sun bursts on the dawn and gives light to the world, so our Lord Jesus, having once burst into our world, majestically, will do it again. In Scripture we are clearly taught that our Lord Jesus, who has come, will also come again. This event is called by many the Second Coming. That is the second tower.

If you have discovered the meaning of grace and the wonder of what God has given you in Christ, then you have responded to his grace and have decided to step off the peninsula and onto the bridge. And as you walk onto the bridge, you will come to that first tower of the epiphany of grace, and you will say, "God, in your great glory and majesty, you have dramatically given us Christ. I put my trust in him." And then you keep on walking across the bridge, looking for the second tower, when the One you have trusted will come again to take you to be with himself for all eternity. This is what Paul in Titus 2:13 calls "the blessed hope."

When the Bible talks about the blessed hope, it doesn't mean wishful thinking. It means the sheer confidence that comes when you know the One whom you have believed. You have stepped off the peninsula, where you had a life characterized by ungodliness and worldly passions anchored in the present day, spewing out wickedness. You have committed yourself to Christ and are starting across the bridge, approaching rapidly that second tower when the great and glorious day of the Lord will come.

The second coming of our Lord Jesus, which we keenly anticipate, is the second tower on which the bridge has been built.

So God's project to deal with his problem people is, first of all, to build two towers: the epiphany of grace and the epiphany of glory, the historical appearance and the eschatological appearance. They are solidly built. One happened; one assuredly will happen. This is the basis of our faith.

Two cables: redemption and sanctification

Suspended on these two towers are two cables on which everything hangs. The first cable is the experience of redemption. Titus 2:14 says that our Lord Jesus, our great God and Savior, "gave himself for us to redeem us from all wickedness." It goes on to say that he gave himself also "to purify for himself a people that are his very own." The second cable is sanctification.

What does redemption mean? Notice that the expression used here, he "gave himself for us to redeem us," is very similar to an expression found in 1 Timothy 2:6—"[He] gave himself as a ransom for all men—the testimony given in its proper time." The idea of redemption, ransom, runs strongly through New Testament teaching. Our Lord Jesus Christ was dealing with a lot of kidnapped people. If we can mix the metaphor, these kidnapped people are on that peninsula. They're stuck out there in their ungodliness and their wickedness. They're drowned by their worldly passions in their present age, and somehow or another, they have to be brought out of the situation they are in.

In addition to the cable of redemption, there is the cable of sanctification. Christ is not just interested in paying a ransom in order that he might release us; he is interested in doing even more than that. He wants to bring us into an experience of sanctification. The term used here is "to purify"—purifying for himself a people that are his very own.

If you look into the expression "a people that are his very own," you find another rich word. It means a very special possession. It's an expression taken from the Old Testament. You can pick it up in

Exodus 19:5, where Jehovah says that the people of Israel are a very special people, uniquely his own. The idea runs right through the Old Testament; and here it's taken up in the New Testament, not speaking of the people of Israel now, but of the church of Jesus Christ.

So when we think of sanctification we have to realize this first of all: When our Lord Jesus works redemption in our lives, he also works sanctification. For if he leads us out of the slave market by paying the ransom, we become his own. Or as the apostle Paul puts it in 1 Corinthians 6:19-20, "You are not your own; you were bought at a price."

That's something God's people have to get hold of. Because, you see, sometimes in our society we invite people to pray to receive Christ. Or we ask people to invite Jesus into their heart. It's relatively easy to get people to pray that prayer or to say they'll ask Jesus into their heart. But that's inadequate. We've got to explain to people, "Listen, if you experience redemption, you're automatically involved in sanctification. For if Christ in redemption pays the ransom for you, then he in sanctification possesses you as his own. You have clearly become his."

The reason I stress this is that you can get people to pray to receive Christ without their having any thought of becoming Christ's; they like to be their own. But you can't swing a bridge on one cable. There is the cable of redemption where we are ransomed, but there is also the cable of sanctification where we are possessed.

In the slave markets in New Testament days, someone would come along and pay the price for a slave. The purchaser would then take the chains off the slave's hands and feet, take him by the hand, and lead him away into a new experience. In other words, he would pay the ransom and take the slave to live in the master's house. What has to be done first? You have to clean him up. There has to be a purifying process. This is all part of the work of the church of Jesus Christ. For sanctification means, on one hand, that we have been set apart for God and we are owned by him; but on the other hand it means that now we're owned by him and we must clean up our act.

So what is God's perfect project? His project is to bridge the gap between where people are and where he wants them to be. How does he do it? First he builds the tower of the appearance of grace—it has happened. Then he builds a second tower, the appearance of glory—it will happen. Then on those two towers he strings the cable of redemption where it is possible for people to be ransomed from their sin and released from their situation; then he strings the cable of sanctification where, having been released from their situation, they become his very own, and he begins to clean up their act. This is the bridge that is being built.

The Walk across the Bridge

We now have people who understand the process and have started on the way, well off the peninsula, but what do we do with them?

Education: edifying and applying

First, the educational process has to be built into people. Paul says the grace of God "teaches us to say 'No' " (Titus 2:12). In other words, when I understand the grace of God, I am exposing myself to the edification process of grace.

I believe that one of the great needs among believers is to understand the grace of God. This idea of God's unmerited favor, his uninhibited giving and unlimited power made available to us for no other reason than that he chose to do it, is something that ought to grip our hearts. It ought to edify our hearts. Why? If I understand that grace led Christ to give himself in my stead and on behalf of me and that it was necessary for him to do this because of my ungodliness, my wickedness, my worldly passions, and my being anchored in the present age, if I understand that, I say, "God, I just can't go back to these worldly passions. God, if grace has brought me out of all that, I can't go back into it." The grace of God has appeared, and because it has burst into my life dramatically, majestically, like the sunrise, it teaches me that I just can't go back to the old life. It teaches me to say no.

This is the beginning of the purification process. This is where some of us need to begin. Some of us need to start taking this more seriously. It is the ultimate insult to God to say that grace redeemed me and took me from where I was, but I don't want to stay here so I spend all my time heading back.

The edification process of grace teaches us to say no to ungodliness and to worldly passions. If we have become utterly riddled with secular thinking and an attitude that doesn't take God seriously, we have to acknowledge that these attitudes are wrong, and every time they appear—because of grace—we'll say no to them. That's the purification process.

Not only that, we've got to learn how to say yes as well—yes to living self-controlled, upright, and godly lives. We've got to say yes to a different attitude toward ourselves, a different attitude toward God, a different attitude toward people.

This is the edification process, and it is the responsibility of the church of Jesus Christ to see that people have entered into it. Grace edifies. God's men and women apply the edification. That's why Paul says in Titus 2:15 that Titus should teach these things—encourage people to say no, rebuke people when they don't say no, and do it with authority. What authority? The authority that comes because you are built on the towers, suspended on the cables, and are on the bridge that God has built.

Expectation

The Bible says that those who believe that Christ will come again believe in a glorious appearing. And there are those who, according to 2 Timothy 4:8, long for his appearing. Some people really get excited about Jesus coming again; sometimes that's because their life down here is so hard they want to get out. I understand that. I don't think that's what Paul is talking about, though. What he's talking about is that we're so excited about the appearing of grace—what happened when Christ first appeared—that we long for his coming and bringing to consummation all that he started, finishing off all that he began. And the thing that really excites us is that while the last time he came it was a crucifixion, the next time he comes it will be a coronation.

Enthusiasm

The expectation of that dramatic, glorious appearing will govern the way we behave. It has a great purifying effect upon us. But then there's the enthusiasm factor, too. For when we understand the bridge and what God has done, when we see what he's done in our lives, then we anticipate with enthusiasm the great and glorious and dreadful day of the Lord. And you know how we show it? We are a people who are eager to do what is good!

If I were to come to you sometime and say, "Tell me, what is your ambition?" I wonder what you'd say. I often ask people, "What would you really like to be?" Do you know what the most beautiful answer could be? "I'd like to be good. I'd really like to be good."

May our Lord grant that we learn to understand his marvelous gift of grace, expect his glorious second coming, and live our lives with the kind of enthusiasm and consistency that makes others want to know why we're different "from the norm."

Perhaps, in his grace and mercy, we may be the very ones to take that person's hand and lead him or her on that "walk across the bridge" to eternal life with God.

Making It Real

1. What is God's people problem? What three terms describe people as God sees us?

2. What are the two towers that hold up the bridge between mankind and God? What are the cables?

3. Are there any parts of the "bridge" that the church ignores today? What would be the danger of missing any one of these parts?

4. The "walk across the bridge" should include education, expectation, and enthusiasm. Which of these need to be emphasized more in the church today?

5. If you could strengthen your understanding of any of the parts of the bridge, which one would you learn more about first? Why?

6
Reminding God's People

Titus 3:1-5

I once read a case history of a man who, because of an error during brain surgery, had the wrong part of his brain removed so that his memory was totally destroyed. He was able to function in all other areas, but without memory. That meant that every time he picked up a newspaper, he read it as if he'd never seen one before. And every time he met a person, he met that person as if he'd never seen him before. Every time he heard a piece of music, he heard it as if hearing it for the first time. Every action he engaged in was as if it had never happened before. Every moment of his life was spent in relearning.

That was quite an arresting thought to me, because I realized how much we depend on memory. If we didn't have memory, we would spend every moment of our lives relearning. But because we do have memory, we can store up the things we have learned; we can accumulate experience. Then we can recall the experience and knowledge we have, and build upon them at any given moment, so that our lives are filled not with relearning but with responding to the accumulation of experience.

Memory enriches our lives unbelievably. However, we do have a problem with memory because, if your memory is like mine, it is the thing we forget with! We forget things for a number of reasons. One of the reasons is that inside the brain there is a slow erosion going on called aging. You may have heard the story of the professor who said to his students, "I'm going to speak to you today on the subject of senility. There are three causes of senility. The first is forgetfulness, and I've forgotten the other two."

Your memory can begin to go because you're getting older, and your memory can also go because you just don't want to remember; we are often capable of putting out of our minds the things we don't want to remember. That is why it is so important to have memory aids built into our lives.

It is interesting to notice how often Scripture insists that, as far as spiritual experience is concerned, we need to go on being reminded. You remember that the Lord Jesus, when he was speaking to his disciples shortly before his departure, told them the Holy Spirit would come and bring things to their remembrance (see John 14:26).

Not only that, Scripture often tells those in positions of Christian leadership that a major part of their responsibility is to go on reminding people. Why? Because if we are to mature spiritually, we do it not by relearning every time we are in a spiritual situation, but by being able to recall the truth and experience we have accumulated over the years. We build on it, and we mature because of our response to it.

Accordingly, the apostle tells Titus it is imperative that he go on reminding the people of certain things. England's Samuel Johnson once said, "It is not adequately understood that men more often need to be reminded than instructed." And, quite frankly, when we look at our own spiritual experience, I think many of us would have to admit that we don't need new experiences, more information, and new truths. What we need is constant reminders to bring experience into line with the truth we have already been given.

Titus 3:1-5 starts off with the word *remind*. In the original language, that word is in the present tense and means, literally, "go on reminding." There are three things in this passage that I want to draw to your attention concerning what we need to be reminded of: how we used to live, how we were saved, and how God's people behave.

How We Used to Live

It is important, said the apostle Paul, to go on reminding people who claim to be disciples of Christ what they used to be like. He is not suggesting to Titus that Christians ought to be constantly raking through the ashes of former experiences, but he is saying that it is healthy for us, if we are maturing spiritually, to have some sense of orientation. And that orientation comes through knowing where we used to be.

Darkened in our understanding

"At one time we too were foolish" (v. 3). That is an expression that talks about our relationship to God. In contemporary idiom, when we talk about people being fools or being foolish, we mean something different from what they meant in New Testament times. Then it meant a person who was devoid of knowledge, of sensitivity as far as God was concerned. You remember the famous expression in the Old Testament that says, "The fear of the LORD is the beginning of knowledge" (Prov. 1:7). In other words, the knowledge of the Lord is the fundamental basis of all real knowledge.

The apostle Paul says to Titus, You and I and all these people in Crete at one time were darkened in our understanding about life. And the reason was that we didn't know God. Because we didn't know God, we didn't understand that all things are created; we didn't know that all things are upheld by his mighty power; we had no sense of purpose; we had no idea of the eternal significance of life. Because we didn't know God, we did not understand our humanity or the reality of relationships. We understood a whole lot of things, but we didn't know God. And in that lack of knowledge of God—or foolishness—we were darkened in every area of our experience.

Many of us can look back to the time when God turned on the lights in our lives and things began to make sense. What was it exactly that turned on the lights? It was the fact that we came to know him. And when his light shone into the darkness of our lives, we realized how utterly dark it had been. "At one time," said the apostle, "we too were foolish." We were darkened in our understanding.

Disobedient to God's truth

There was also a time when we were disobedient, says Paul. We can be disobedient to God in a lot of ways. Simply reading the things that come from God's Word and saying, "I don't believe that. I don't buy that. I don't want anything to do with that. I am simply going to ignore it," is being disobedient.

There are other people who will say, "Well, I believe that's what God says, and I believe that's what I ought to do, but quite frankly, there are other considerations, and I don't want to do what God says; I much prefer to do what I want to do." That's also disobedience.

There is also a sense in which if I live in self-induced ignorance of what God says, I am engaging in disobedience. The particular situation of the person who is brought up in a Christianized, Westernized society, where he is constantly exposed to the opportunity of reading the Word of God and countless other books, Christian newspapers, and periodicals and hearing Christian radio and watching Christian television and still doesn't bother to find out what God says—this person is living in rank disobedience to what God says. And many of us can look back on the time when we lived in self-induced ignorance of what God says.

Deceived by misinformation

Then Paul goes on to talk about relation to self. At one time we too were "deceived and enslaved by all kinds of passions and pleasures." Deceived, he says, by misinformation.

It would be easy for us to point out the time in our lives when God's truth burst into our consciousness and we began to understand how utterly wrong we had been about God and about everything. If I'm wrong about God, I'm wrong about the world, I'm wrong about humanity, I'm wrong about society. If I'm wrong about God, I'm wrong about reality, period. This is an overwhelming thought, but it happens to be true. If I am wrong about God, it means that I have developed a philosophy of life and a lifestyle that I think is right, but it is only when God shines his truth into my life that I understand I lived all those years deceived by error. What I thought was truth wasn't truth at all. What I thought was reality was fantasy. What I thought was the way to go was actually the way to destruction.

Scripture says, "There is a way that seems right to a man, but in the end it leads to death" (Prov. 14:12). It is important to remind people that they, before they knew the Lord and acknowledged Christ as Savior and Lord, were living lives that, in relation to God, were characterized by darkness and disobedience. But as far as their own souls were concerned, their lives were characterized by utter deception. They had been sent all kinds of misinformation by the enemy of their souls, and they got just about everything wrong.

Frequently people say to me, "You know, I look at my life, and I can't believe how many things I've gotten wrong. I can't believe how many wrong decisions I've made and how many situations I've gotten myself into that are an unbelievable mess." Why is that? It's because they were living their lives estranged from God and his truth. They were deceived by the enemy of their souls.

Dominated by self-centeredness

Notice that Paul also says we were dominated by self-interest. We were "deceived and enslaved by all kinds of passions and pleasures." People think that pleasure is great; they are all in favor of indulging in their own passions. And our present society advocates: "Get as much pleasure as you can; if it feels good, do it." But what they don't say is what the Bible tells us: You live a life indulging in your passions, solely interested in your own pleasures, and you'll end up enslaved by your own passions and pleasures. That's what Paul is saying in Titus 3:3.

Scripture has something powerful to say to us that is in total contrast to what we are hearing all around us. Our society tells us that our passions are our own business and that we should indulge in them—the important thing is our pleasure and that if something gives us pleasure, it must be good.

Scripture says that if you go that way, indulging in your passions, being solely interested in your pleasures, you will end up utterly a slave to these things.

That's exactly what our society is telling us to do. They are insisting on sexual freedom. What they don't tell us is that if we go on engaging in what is euphemistically called sexual freedom, alternate lifestyles—whatever terms you want to use—we will end up a slave to our own passions, because we'll be totally consumed by the desire to satisfy ourselves. And if pleasure is the watchword of our lives, and we can only be happy when we are having a pleasurable experience, then we must never be bored and never engage in anything mundane or routine. If that's the way we're going to live, we're going to have to spend all our time, money, and energy trying to avoid living in the real world, and we become enslaved by our desire to escape reality.

That's where we used to be—utterly dominated by our own desire for pleasure, by our insistence on the freedom to indulge in our own passions. And it was captivating, dominating, enslaving.

Distorted in relationships

If my relationship to God is wrong, my relationship to myself will be wrong. And if my relationship to myself is wrong, then my relationship to other people is going to be all wrong, too. The person who is only interested in his own passions and pleasures doesn't make a very good husband. The person who is only interested in making sure that she's always happy and always looked after doesn't make a very good wife or mother. And the person who is totally self-absorbed makes a rotten employee, and an even worse employer.

In other words, if I get myself wrong with God, I've got myself wrong with me, and I've got myself wrong with people all over the place. Look at what Paul goes on to say: "At one time we too were foolish, disobedient" (that's toward God), and "deceived and enslaved by all kinds of passions and pleasures" (that's as far as myself is concerned). Accordingly, he goes on: "We lived in malice and envy, being hated and hating one another." How true many of us know this to be.

But we have to look into our own lives and say that our relationships to others have been totally distorted because our reactions to them have not been what they ought to be. For example, we got married, and what were we interested in? Love? No. Passion. We got married, and what were we concerned about? Commitment till death parts us? No. Our own pleasure is all we were interested in. We weren't interested in what God said about marriage. And we weren't interested in what God said about family.

If I lived my life making sure that I was always happy and my passions were always dealt with, I would become unbelievably malicious whenever another person wouldn't do as I wanted him to do. And this leads to hatred. What passes for marriage today in our society is often a cruel parody of what marriage is intended to be. What passes for families in many areas of society today are obscene caricatures of what family is supposed to be. How do we account for this dichotomy? Because we are wrong as far as God is concerned; we're all wrong in our relationship with ourselves; therefore, we cannot have proper relationships with one another.

Can you look back to a time when you used to be like the person I just described? More importantly, can you now look at yourself and see the difference? That brings us to the second point. We are to go on reminding people not only of how they used to live, but how they were saved.

How We Were Saved

But is one of my favorite words in the Bible; it's an important one. When you see a *but,* always put a circle around it, because it is going to lead to a stark contrast to what has just been said. We used to be this way at one time, Paul says, and then he goes on and says *but*.

There was a famous preacher in London, Dr. Martin Lloyd-Jones, who was preaching through Romans, and when he came to "But God," I think he spent two months just sermonizing on that little phrase. I promise to be briefer!

"But when the kindness and love of God our Savior appeared, he saved us" (3:4-5). Why do we have to go on reminding ourselves of how we used to live? Because if we can go on reminding ourselves of how we used to live, we can start getting excited all over again about how God saved us.

Through an act of God

First, *salvation is an act* of God as our Savior on our behalf, not an action of man. Verses 4 and 5 say that "when the kindness and love of God our Savior appeared, he saved us, not because of righteous things we had done, but because of his mercy."

You can know God in many capacities: Father, Creator, Maker, Judge, Sustainer, Shepherd, and so on. But you must know him as Savior, the one who intervened in your affairs and did something about your sins. He needs to be known as Savior, the one who moved into your life and changed you from what you were into what you are.

Why did he do it? Because you deserved it? No. Because you merited it? No. Because it was your idea that he should do it? No. Why then did he do it? Because of loving-kindness and tender mercy and unmerited grace. Being changed from what you were into what you are is something that's attributable to God, and to God alone.

We have been brainwashed into thinking that if anything is going to be achieved in our lives, we're going to have to do it ourselves. Well, get this straight if you've never gotten it straight before. You can't save yourself!

Some years ago in England I led a conference for some bored teenagers. It was a typical English summer's day, with lots of *liquid* sunshine pouring out of the skies. We had about five hundred kids there just hanging around and looking out the windows at the rain, bored to tears. I figured I had to do something, so I brought a bucket into the middle of the room. Then I said there was a pound note, a nice, crisp, green pound note, for the first kid who could stand in the bucket and lift himself off the ground. They thought that was the easiest pound they would ever earn in their lives. Kept them happy all afternoon, trying to earn their pound. And I've still got the pound, because you can't lift yourself off the ground standing in your own bucket. Neither can you save yourself. It's an act of God, who intervenes.

God in his loving-kindness, tender mercy, and capacity as Savior has moved into our lives and has done something for us we couldn't do for ourselves. Notice how Paul puts it in verse 4: "When the kindness and love of God our Savior appeared."

Remember the suspension bridge? Remember how God has appeared and how he will appear; and how that first dramatic appearance, or epiphany, was the appearance of grace, when God appeared in the person of Christ, like the dawn bursting onto the horizon and banishing the darkness? In Christ, he appeared. He lived on earth; he died on the cross; he rose again and returned to heaven. That is the first glorious appearing of God our Savior. In Christ's death and resurrection, God has done for us what we couldn't do for ourselves. He saved us. And God's people know what they used to be, but they also know they've been saved through an act of God.

Through a fact

Second, *salvation is a fact*. "He saved us" (v. 5). Salvation is not something you sort of feel and then you don't feel. Salvation is something that is rooted in history. It is rooted in the appearance of God our Savior in the person of Christ. Jesus Christ really was born. He really did live. He really did die. He really did rise again. He demonstrated that he was the Son of God with authority by rising from the dead; and he offers us salvation.

Salvation is something that is factual. It is verifiable because it happened in history; it happened in time; it happened in space; it isn't just a theological concept; it isn't just a metaphysical experience. It is a fact. Christ appeared and died and rose again for our salvation. And we can go on reminding ourselves of this. God acted, and we can be sure of it!

It was interesting to notice that the tense of the Greek that is used for *saved* in verse 5 is the aorist, which means it is an accomplished fact. He has specifically, definitely, incontrovertibly saved us.

Through a promise

Third, *salvation is a pact* where God makes an agreement with us. He says to us, "If you will come in repentance and faith and allow me to do for you what you can't do for yourself; if you'll allow me to reach over and get hold of the bucket—that situation in which you find yourself—and allow me in Christ to pick you up when you can't pick yourself up, I promise to do it. I promise to save you from your sins. I promise to save you from your self-centeredness. I promise to save you from the consequence of your sins. I promise to save you from a lost eternity." We are supposed to go on reminding people of this.

I find many people are reluctant to say boldly, "I have been saved." I could never understand why. Are you reluctant to say that? Let me remind you, you are supposed to be able to say it because you know it. And you know it because God acted. He showed you that your salvation is a fact. He has made a pact with you that if you will come in repentance and faith, he will save you.

How can I know I'm saved? I can know initially because I take God at his word and believe and trust him. But then I can know more definitely as time goes on because I continue to take him at his word.

How God's People Behave

It's one thing to say I've been saved, to be able to say God reached into my life and did for me what I couldn't do for myself. But we've got to be able to substantiate it. And we do that by the way we behave. God's people behave differently from those who are not God's people. That should be so obvious it ought not to be necessary to say. But we do need to go on reminding each other of this. Why? Because behaving differently from people who are not God's people is hard. And because it's hard, we forget.

Behaving differently means that we cannot indulge ourselves the way we used to do, and we want to indulge ourselves, so we carefully forget. Behaving differently means that I reject the things that many of my friends stand for. It means that I refuse to be what they insist I be, and that's going to mean some estrangement. So what do I do? I forget.

One of the greatest tragedies of the Christian church in North America is that millions of people profess they have been saved but show absolutely no evidence of it, because they insist on living the way the unsaved do. And many of the thinking people in the church are saying that one of the great tragedies of the contemporary American church is that we've got the manpower, we've got the woman-power, but we don't have the dynamic to change our society. Why is that?

If we want to be saved but don't want to be different, we won't change anything. The apostle said, "Remind the people to be subject to rulers and authorities, to be obedient, to be ready to do whatever is good, to slander no one, to be peaceable and considerate, and to show true humility toward all men" (Titus 3:1-2).

Respect authority

First of all, the behavior of God's people is supposed to be different as they relate to authority. I hate to see a kid who professes to be a

Christian argue with a referee. That turns me right off. He shows no respect for authority. I hate to see people who profess to be believers refusing to accept God-ordained authority in the fellowship of believers. I really get perturbed about people who profess to be believers but have no readiness to accept the legal authorities of their society. They won't go along with the laws of the land; they resist them or break them as far as they can get away with it. Let's face it: One of the ways we are going to show that we are saved is to show a respectful attitude toward authority.

There's a rotten attitude toward authority in our society today. You see it in sports; you see it in the way we drive our cars; you see it in just about every stratum of society and every aspect of our lives. One of the ways that Christians show themselves different is by the respect they have for authority. Why? Because authority is God-ordained. It doesn't mean that we have to agree with the authority. It doesn't mean the authority is always right. But it does mean that God has ordained authority and we will respond to authority properly because we believe that all authority has its ultimate source in God himself. God's people need to be reminded to behave differently in terms of authority.

Be charitable

Remind the people "to be ready to do whatever is good." Whenever Christians have the opportunity to do something good and kind and charitable, they should be there on the front line. Look at the many charitable things that are going on in our society, the many attempts that are being made to assist people who are in deep need. Remarkably, often we can't find believers who want to be involved in that kind of thing. Why? Because they haven't been prepared to be saved enough from their self-centeredness to get into volunteering to help somebody else. But what an impact it makes when believers begin to understand that saved people have a different attitude toward authority and a healthy attitude toward charity.

Behave with integrity

Remind the people "to slander no one, but to be peaceable and considerate, and to show true humility toward all men." That means saying what is true and only speaking what is necessary. One of the most dangerous weapons we have in our arsenal today is our tongue. What we say about people and what we say about each other is often not true, certainly not necessary, and terribly damaging. I don't know how many hours I've spent in my pastorate trying to heal wounds that have been caused by someone's tongue. And, quite frankly, most of the things that were said were certainly not necessary, and many of the things that were said just weren't true. There was an incredible lack of integrity on the part of the person who spoke the words.

Treat others with dignity

Jill caught the limousine to the airport in Tucson, Arizona, one day. The limousine hardly looked like a limousine; it was a beat-up old van. Jill and six men were the passengers, with a glamorous driver. Probably because the van was so beat up, the limousine company provided a glamorous driver. Anyway, the vehicle quit after a few blocks and the six men started raising Cain because they wanted to get to their planes. The driver couldn't fix the van, so Jill asked, "What are we going to do?"

The driver said, "You're just going to have to flag down a cab."

Jill told the others she had an early flight—in fact, hers was the first flight of all seven of them. A cab came along, and three of the men piled in and took off. Another cab came along, and the other three men piled in and took off. Jill was left there on her own, sitting inside the van.

I have no idea why these men acted with such discourtesy. Perhaps they felt so many women have screamed about equality for so long, they just decided to give it to them. Much can be said on both sides of the issue, but one thing is not up for debate, and that is that

Christians do not behave like that—Christians feel a deep sense of dignity for all people. Christians are considerate people, courteous people, gentle people, and meek people. In other words, Christians treat people with dignity. We need to keep reminding each other of that!

Making It Real

1. Why is it important for Christians to be reminded of what they used to be like?

2. Explain the author's statement that: "not all people are God's people, but all God's people are saved people." Is this an "acceptable" statement in our society today? Why, or why not?

3. How should God's people behave differently from those who are not his people?

4. How does your behavior serve to substantiate your salvation and relationship to God:

   —In your home?

   —In your church?

   —In your community?

   —In your workplace?

7

Motivating God's People

Titus 3:5-8

One of the great themes that occurs over and over again in this brief Epistle is that those who are believers behave in a specific and special way. And one of the unique aspects of the behavior of believers is that they demonstrate their relationship to the Lord to a great extent by the way they treat people. We find a constant emphasis that if you are a believer, you are committed in your society to living a life of doing good.

One of the problems of religious experience, however, is that it's difficult for some people to get around to being spiritually motivated. There are a number of reasons for this. Because there are so many demands on our time and resources, we have a problem juggling all these things and keeping all our balls in the air. Often the ball that gets dropped is involvement in our religious or spiritual experience.

This is not true for all people. For instance, there are some people who are unbelievably devoted to religious activity. They are phenomenally motivated, devoting their whole lives to it. They will give up everything, making vows and commitments, to the extent that it becomes obvious that absolutely nothing else matters except their spiritual experience. But if you evaluate their motivation, often you discover the reason for that assiduous motivation, determination, and overwhelming devotion is that they are working on the assumption that if they are devoted enough, busy enough, and motivated enough, then hopefully everything will work out in the end and they will be saved; they will come into an experience of the living God.

In other words, there are a lot of people who are highly motivated in the religious realm, hoping they will be saved as a reward.

The problem with this motivation is that Scripture tells us repeatedly that salvation is not a reward for a highly motivated or a highly devoted life. Over and over again we see in Scripture, not the least in the Epistle to Titus, that the principle of salvation is not that God saves us because of the righteous things we have done. On the contrary, the righteous things we have done are, in God's sight, "like filthy rags" (Isa. 64:6). They are not going to earn salvation.

Accordingly, Christian leaders have a big problem. If people have a hard time being religiously motivated—and then only for a reward—and you take away the possibility of reward, how on earth are you going to keep them involved and motivated? How are you going to get them inspired to do anything at all? This is one of the great problems confronting the Christian church today.

Everybody in the pastorate is aware of this problem. That's why you find a variety of methodologies to motivate people who know they are not going to be saved because of what they do, and, therefore, are not particularly interested in doing anything at all.

Some preachers share their great burden and plead with people. Often the pleading works with one or two rather sensitive souls, but on the whole it doesn't make any difference. Another approach is to threaten, "I'm going to do this if you don't do this." But people do as they want to anyway; threats don't make any difference. Another is to challenge them to do certain things. But it's amazing how, if you challenge people long enough, they become totally inoculated against it.

So pleading doesn't work; threatening doesn't work; challenging doesn't work; offering an ultimatum doesn't work; offering rewards only works so long. What on earth, then, can we do to get people motivated?

That is one of the most important questions we can ever deal with in Scripture, and Paul gives the answer here: He tells Titus how he is to motivate the people in Crete to live lives of goodness, challenge, commitment, and involvement.

Where Salvation Originates

First of all, we have to notice that Paul's emphasis, as far as his ministry is concerned, is teaching. He is constantly underscoring the spiritual truths that are important. It seems to me that over and over again the apostle Paul is not so much pleading or threatening or challenging people as he is teaching them. And he seems to have tremendous confidence that when people are properly and adequately taught there will be an assimilation of truth, which will become a fuel of motivation in their lifestyle. Motivating includes underscoring what is important.

And what is it that Paul teaches? You'll notice that the apostle is very careful to go on stressing, almost *ad nauseam,* that salvation is not the product of human activity, but that it originates with God.

The grace of God

Even as I've written this exposition of the Word of God as found in Titus, I realize how deep-rooted the idea is that salvation is the product of the way we live. We have to go on stressing that this is one of the most fundamental errors in human thinking; it is rooted in· human pride. We believe that we are the circumference of all things. Deep down, we really believe that we have the solution to all things, that somehow or another everything depends on us, that even our spiritual relationship is fundamentally dependent upon our doing things right so that God can respond.

But salvation, Scripture tells us, originates with the grace of God. Titus 3:7 states categorically that we are justified by his grace. Verse 4 tells us that "the kindness and love of God our Savior appeared" so that he might save us "because of his mercy" (v. 5). If you experience salvation, it is totally attributable to the grace, mercy, and loving-kindness of God. It started there because God wanted to give to you what you didn't deserve. This is utterly fundamental to the uniqueness of Christianity.

The person of Jesus Christ

Second, Paul stresses that salvation *appears in the person of Jesus Christ*. In verse 6, Paul says the Holy Spirit was "poured out on us generously through Jesus Christ our Savior." In Titus 2:13 he speaks of a "glorious appearing" of our Lord Jesus. Our salvation, originating with the grace of God, is made available to us exclusively in our Lord Jesus Christ.

It's remarkable that there are still people in our churches who think they can be saved in all kinds of different ways, that it doesn't really matter what you believe as long as you are sincere. And there are people who have heard the preaching of the Word of God for weeks and months, some of them for years, and the fact of salvation still has not clicked. That is why people aren't interested in missions. They still think it doesn't matter about those who know nothing of Christ; they're not really lost. They don't see why it's important that people should give of themselves to take the message of Christ to those who have never heard. They don't think it's important because they don't accept the fact that Scripture tells us that salvation is available in Jesus Christ exclusively; there is salvation in none other.

The outpouring of the Holy Spirit

Third, our salvation originates in *the outpouring of the Holy Spirit*. Salvation comes in different tenses. There is the past tense, in which we can say we "have been saved." There's the future tense, in which we look forward with confidence and say we "will be saved." And there is the present tense, in which we can look at our daily experience and say we "are being saved." In all these dimensions the Holy Spirit is at work.

Do you know why you were saved? You were saved because the grace of God—an attitude of God—took the initiative and provided

Christ for you, a Christ you couldn't provide for yourself. Do you know how you came to understand and respond to the message of Christ? The Spirit of God opened your blind eyes, touched your hard heart, moved your chloroformed conscience, and began to allow you to understand the depth of your own sin and the wonder of Christ's glory. And now you can look back on your past and say, "I used to be like that, but I'm not anymore" because the Holy Spirit, who opened your eyes has now come into your heart and is slowly transforming you into the image of Christ. *You* didn't open your eyes. It wasn't through your remarkable capabilities. It wasn't through your great rational intelligence that you were able to grasp the immensity of truth. It was the work of the Holy Spirit—inspiring Scripture, inspiring preacher and witness, working in your own heart, bringing conviction and understanding—that brought you to salvation.

If we're going to motivate people properly in the Christian church, we have to do it by getting them to understand that our salvation originated with the grace of God through the appearing of Christ in the outpouring of the Holy Spirit. It wasn't you or I who did it. It was all of grace, mercy, and divine initiative. That has to be fundamental in our understanding.

What Salvation Incorporates

The washing of rebirth

In verse 5, Paul talks about the washing of rebirth. This expression immediately suggests two things to me. First of all, the word *washing* speaks of the necessity of cleansing from defilement. *Rebirth* speaks of the opportunity for a fresh beginning. Theologians have had a marvelous time disagreeing over this expression. We won't get into the area of disagreement, but will concentrate on the thrust of the passage to help us understand how to motivate God's people—by making sure they understand the things that are important.

One of the important things is that when we are saved, we have been cleansed from past defilement and introduced into an experience where we have the priceless privilege of a fresh beginning. There are some who rejoice in this. There are people who are rather like the sinful woman who came to our Lord Jesus, when he was at the banquet table, and put the precious ointment on his feet, weeping and wiping her tears from his feet with her hair. And when people criticized her for such "unbecoming" behavior, our Lord Jesus said, "Her many sins have been forgiven—for she loved much" (Luke 7:47).

I've observed that often people who understand that salvation means a washing, a cleansing, a blotting out of their past are people who are the most highly motivated in Christian service. Those who have been forgiven much, more often than not, are the ones who love much. Those who understand the depth of their sin are the ones who get excited about the wonder of their cleansing. They are so excited about it they want to take every opportunity to express thanksgiving.

The washing of rebirth also speaks of a new beginning. The theme of being born again—literally "regeneration," a new genesis, a new beginning—is found in many parts of Scripture. It's a delightful theme.

There are many people who talk about their past with a note of despair. They wonder how on earth anything good could ever come out of their lives. But the great message of the Christian gospel is that God is prepared to move into the most broken life and give it a new genesis. And the wonder of this new beginning is that Christ becomes our Savior and Lord, and the Holy Spirit is poured out generously upon us and becomes the dynamic of a whole new experience.

Think of how new a beginning this is. Up until that time you steered your own ship, you paddled your own canoe. Up until that time you went down the rapids of society and came up against the rocks and the boulders; you were swamped and bruised and were sinking. But then something dramatic happened. You turned the control of your canoe over to the Lord, a mighty Holy Spirit, who was able to get into the situation and take charge. That's the new beginning.

The apostle Paul says it is imperative that we stress these things to people so they can understand that salvation incorporates cleansing from past defilements and the opportunity for a fresh beginning.

Now then, some of you are still saying, "What's the controversy in all this?" The controversy stems from the word *washing*. Many commentators—probably most commentators—say this means that through baptism you are regenerated and through baptism you have this renewal.

One branch of Christendom interprets it as follows: If a person goes through the experience of baptism, that automatically—almost in a mechanical sense—ensures that the person is regenerated and renewed. Let me take this to its most extreme position. When Jill was about to produce our third child, Peter, she was having all kinds of problems. Peter wasn't too enthusiastic about coming into this cold world. He has always been very fond of his own comforts, and we should have realized way back then what he was going to be like. He was in no hurry at all. He was laid-back then; just as he is laid-back now. Eventually, however, he arrived on the scene, but only after numerous false alarms and much consternation on the part of those who were caring for Jill and the unborn baby.

A nurse who was looking after Jill said to me, "Do you realize that there is a very real possibility that this baby might die?"

And I answered, "Yes, I fully realize that is a possibility."

"Well," she said, "what steps have you taken to baptize this baby the moment it is born?"

I said, "None whatsoever."

She said, "I think you are grossly out of order. I cannot believe that anybody would have such an attitude, and I insist that you make arrangements for somebody to be here so that the moment that baby is born, it can be baptized."

So I said, "Why?"

"Because if the baby is not baptized and dies, the baby will go to hell."

So I said, "But if the baby is baptized what will happen?"

"He'll go to heaven."

"In other words," I said, "he's going to be saved by baptism?"

She said, "Exactly."

And I said, "Well, madam, with all due respect, you're exactly wrong."

"No, you're exactly wrong." And she went on, "I'm going to tell you something. If you don't make arrangements to have the baby baptized, I will baptize the baby myself."

And I said, "God bless you. Go right ahead."

"Well," she said, "That is not really what you ought to do. You ought to have a minister come in and do it."

This lady was deeply sincere. She could have appealed, if she'd known the Bible, to Titus 3:5 and other similar verses. And she could have said, "Listen. It is through the washing that rebirth and renewal takes place. It is through baptism."

What we've got to point out, however, is this: Nowhere does Scripture teach that regeneration, renewal, and reconciliation to God are the results of a mechanical application of a rite. Rather, Scripture teaches that regeneration and renewal are the result of people responding in faith to the grace of God.

Sometimes you'll find that all God does is spoken of as being related to faith, and other times you'll find it is related to baptism. In other words Scripture says that people are regenerated and renewed through faith in the grace of God, and incorporated in this whole act of faith is the act of baptism. Not that baptism, in an automatic, mechanical sense, will produce salvation without faith, but that faith will also require a person to take a stand as far as his relationship with Christ is concerned, and part of that stand is experiencing baptism.

I may be writing to some who think you can be saved through baptism alone. But you are overlooking the whole thrust of this passage, which says that we are justified by grace, and it is those who believe in God who are saved.

Second, if you are a believer, but have not recognized the significance of baptism, you need to take another hard look at it.

Because if you have not, in one mode or another, experienced baptism, this is something that ought to be done.

Renewal by the Holy Spirit

Also in verse 5, we see that salvation incorporates renewal by the Holy Spirit. This idea of renewal is another beautiful theme in Scripture. For instance, we are told in Colossians 3:10 that when we come to faith in Christ, we are made a new person. The old person is gone; the new person has been made in the image of Christ. We are told in Romans 12:2 that we have a new mind that is constantly being renewed. And we are told in 2 Corinthians 4:16 that even though our outward body is wasting away—that means our hair is dropping out, our skin is getting all kinds of wrinkles, and whatever we do to make it appear that this is not the case, it is the case—our inner man is being renewed. What does this mean?

It means that when I come to faith in Christ, God gives me the opportunity to be a new person. He will draw the drapes on the old person. The old person, as Paul says in Romans 6:4, has been buried with Christ in baptism. We died with Christ in order that we might be raised into newness of life with Christ.

This is one of the most exciting things you can tell people, particularly those who would love to be able to walk away from their past, to feel that God can renew them and give them the opportunity to do something positive after having had a long career of doing that which is negative. That is exactly what he is saying here: It is possible for us to be renewed by the Holy Spirit, to be made a new person, to be able to walk away from our old self, to have a new mind—which means a new attitude—and to have this attitude constantly renewed. And even though outwardly we are fading away, inwardly there is renewal, refreshing, strengthening. The older we get, the more refreshing and the more renewed we become. That's what God does in salvation, if we respond in faith to his grace.

Justification by grace

In verse 7 Paul talks about being justified by his grace. The word *justified* is related to the word *righteousness*. The Bible teaches the righteousness of God, which means, among other things, that he is always right.

Now, in sharp contrast to the sinlessness of the always-rightness of God, people are sinful and have done things that are unrighteous. And the big human dilemma is, how can an unrighteous person find his or her way into the presence of a righteous God? The answer is only through the justification that stems from the grace of God.

What is justification? Justification means literally that God declares me right with him. It's a legal term. It's like I'm on trial and God is sitting on the bench as my judge. The charge is made against me—what I've been, what I've done—the whole sordid thing is there. All the evidence comes out. It is irrefutable; there's not a thing I can do about it. There I am before a holy, absolutely just God, and he knows everything about me. He hears all there is to hear about me and then he pronounces the verdict, which is a foregone conclusion: Guilty. Of course I'm guilty before the eyes of a righteous God.

What then can I do? I can stand there and simply admit my guilt. I can bring out the petty little things I have done in my religious observance in my halfhearted "good life." But it has a hollow sound in the courtroom of God, who listens to it all and pronounces me guilty nevertheless. And I know it is true; I am guilty.

God sentences me, but then he does the most remarkable thing. He takes off his robe of office, steps down, and himself pays the fine. And having offered me the payment for the fine, he then goes back to the bench, puts on his robes, and declares something that is music to my ears: "This person before me is utterly unrighteous; I, the righteous God, have found him guilty. The judgment has been passed, but the penalty has been paid. I paid it myself, and therefore I, the righteous judge, proclaim him free. I proclaim him without any further obligation before me. I declare him righteous—justified."

Will you come to that court and say, "Whew, what a good thing I joined the church and started tithing when I was forty-five. Wow, if I hadn't started tithing, I'd never have made it up here to heaven. What a good thing I was kind to my aged mother when she was eighty-three. That brought me here"? No, you won't say any of that. You will walk out of that courtroom and say, "I'm utterly unrighteous before a righteous God. But he rightly found me guilty, paid the penalty himself in his precious Son, our Lord Jesus, and offered me what I couldn't earn for myself, and by faith I took it. He donned his robes of office again and declared me righteous." Why? Grace! And don't ever forget it.

The apostle Paul, having explained all this in the Epistle to the Romans, asks, "Where, then, is boasting?" And I love his response. "It is excluded" (Rom. 3:27). One of the nice things about heaven is that nobody will be bragging because there will be nobody there who has anything to brag about. The only people in heaven will be those who have been justified freely by his grace; who have been regenerated; who have been renewed and made heirs of eternal life.

Grace makes salvation available. The empty hand of repentant faith makes salvation actual, and those who are thus justified, out of gratitude are deeply motivated to honor their Savior and Lord.

True Motivation

Okay, so I've got my theology straight, I understand how salvation works and how I became rightly related with God. But once I've done that, there is an ethical demand upon me. I'm supposed to behave a certain way now that I'm a believer. I ought to do some things, and ought not to do other things. This is what we call the ethics of Christianity. How can we get people to do what they should and to stop doing what they should not do? We can do it when people are so caught up in the theology of grace that they grasp the ethics of gratitude. When I'm overwhelmed with the goodness and unmerited favor of God, I will have an overwhelming sense of gratitude, and I will exhibit it by being what God wants me to be. Therein lies the purest motivation for the Christian.

You can threaten them as long as you like. You can plead with them as much as you want. You can challenge them till you're blue in the face. But I have come to the conviction that, in the long run, while all these things may well have their valid place in terms of motivation, the primary motivation is that people begin to understand that it is the grace of God alone that brings salvation, and it is gratitude to God that motivates them to live as they should.

That's why when people come to me and talk about their Christian motivation, I usually, to their surprise, go back to the beginning and try to make sure that they understand the simple message of the grace of God. When I remember where I was until God in his grace touched me, I have no difficulty recognizing where people are, and that motivates me toward them.

I hear people talking about burnout. I've heard of burned-out nurses, burned-out teachers, and even burned-out preachers!

I get alarmed when I hear about burned-out preachers, because it seems to me that any preacher who understands the grace of God and remembers where he used to be should have adequate resources of grace to keep him encouraged and enabled for the ministry of grace. Of course there are other considerations that need to be taken into account, but generally speaking, an adequate grasp of grace should keep all of us on the job. "This is a trustworthy saying. And I want you to stress these things, so that those who have trusted in God may be careful to devote themselves to doing what is good. These things are excellent and profitable for everyone" (Titus 3:8). As we think in terms of motivating people in the Christian church, we're not thinking so much of pleading; we're not thinking so much of challenging. We're thinking primarily of teaching. Teaching people: underscoring what is important in such a way that the people understand the significance of it, so that eventually they will respond to it appropriately. And what is the appropriate response? An utter devotion to what is good and a tremendous desire for what is excellent before God.

It is up to the individual believer to discover in the context of the fellowship of believers the good works for which he was redeemed, and then to do them wholeheartedly as unto the Lord. This honors God, blesses those who are ministered to, and wonderfully enriches the involved believer.

Making It Real

1. Why is lack of motivation one of the great problems confronting the Christian church today?

2. Where does salvation originate? How does our society react to this information? Why? How do Christians show we struggle with it as well?

3. Which people best understand the "washing of rebirth"? What is the outcome of this understanding?

4. What is the best method of motivation for Christian service? What motivates you personally?

8
Warning God's People

Titus 3:8-15

*I*t is important that we recognize the place of the local church in the economy of God. Viewed from the human point of view, the local church is a gathering of people who have in common their relationship to the Lord Jesus. And as we have seen in this Epistle, viewed from the divine perspective, the local church is called God's very own people.

Because you have the privilege in your local church of being God's very own people, you also have a corresponding responsibility. And that is you should not only live individually in such a way that people know you belong to the Lord Jesus, but you should also live corporately as his children. Not only is our world going to look at the behavior of individuals to get a feel for who Christ is, but our world should also be able to look at a corporate group of people, a body of believers, in order that they might see what is different about Christians. And let's face it, a person who is not a believer wants to know if Christian theology is for real. A person who is not a believer wants to know what it is that makes believers so different.

One of the best ways to show the difference is by pointing to the local church and then by pointing out how they behave corporately in a way that is different from other groups of people in our society. What a pressing responsibility it is, not only to be a believer, but to be a member of the local fellowship, a member of the church of Christ.

With all that in mind, we come to a rather solemn final word from the apostle Paul.

Warning: Division in the Church Cannot Be Accepted

Look at Titus 3:10: "Warn a divisive person once, and then warn him a second time. After that, have nothing to do with him." And if you're not sure what that means, this may help: strike one; strike two; you're out! Perhaps that's a rather crude way of putting it, but the apostle Paul speaks so forcibly, so seriously, so solemnly about division in the church of Jesus Christ that he says it's totally unacceptable.

I think one of the weaknesses of the church in the contemporary setting is that we have become soft in the whole area of division. We have not realized how serious it is for people who profess to be a body of believers to live in such a way that it is perfectly obvious they are not a body. Often we simply paint over the cracks; we whitewash the situation, hoping it will go away; or we pretend it never came about. As a result, in many instances, the church of Jesus Christ loses her credibility. That's why we need to read carefully what the apostle is saying.

How Do Divisions Come About?

What do we mean by a division in the church, and how does it come about? Notice, in verse 9, that Paul tells Titus and the people to whom he is ministering to "avoid foolish controversies."

An issue is raised

The Greek word for "controversy" has its roots in the word for "to seek." I have a feeling that most controversies start because people are interested enough in a topic to seek out what is really involved. They get involved and start studying it with increasing intensity.

Then they bump up against somebody who doesn't necessarily see eye-to-eye with them, and they start debating.

But then, in the New Testament, the word that started out "to seek" and then became "debate" eventually degenerated into "controversy." The apostle Paul is talking specifically about controversies here in Titus. Notice the adjective he uses to describe them. He talks about *"foolish* controversies."

People seek to know the truth of a matter; then other people will see different sides of it, and inevitably this results in debates and discussions. However, these discussions and debates can become controversial. When those controversies become "foolish controversies," you have the seeds of a division. And the apostle Paul says to watch it carefully, indeed.

An emphasis is introduced

"Avoid foolish controversies and genealogies." When Paul wrote to Timothy in Ephesus, as well as to Titus in Crete, he pointed out that they were going to have trouble with what he calls in another place "endless genealogies." What were they? There were certain teachers who would take some of the genealogies of the Old Testament and decide they weren't complete enough. So they began to fill in the cracks—or what they thought were cracks—with all kinds of myths. As a result, they would produce the most fanciful ideas imaginable; then they would spend all their time discussing and debating the particular things that were of interest to them.

I don't know if you have noticed this, but in the church of Jesus Christ, it is easy to get interested in an *emphasis*. Always remember that an emphasis unrelated to the corresponding emphasis of Scripture is the breeding ground for a heresy. One of the problems in our contemporary church is that emphases become fads. It has been suggested that perhaps one of the most chronic ills of the contemporary church in North America at the present time is "fadism." It isn't that we're into endless genealogies; rather, we're not satisfied with what Scripture says so we have to fill in what we feel it should have said and build up and emphasize the whole thing and get gung-ho about it. We push it to such lengths that we can no longer substantiate it from Scripture. As a result, we begin to muddy the waters. This kind of a situation, coupled with foolish controversies, can be ecclesiastical dynamite. It can be the beginning of a division in the church.

People react

"Avoid foolish controversies and genealogies and arguments." The word translated *argument* here is translated *strife* in other parts of Scripture—people getting into these emphases, into these positions, into these situations, and getting thoroughly upset about it. Instead of having harmony in the church, instead of really being united in being what they are called to be, people get themselves absorbed with the issues.

The apostle says to watch out for this. He gives us an example of this kind of thing in 1 Corinthians 3:1-4 as he addresses the church in Corinth, which was a model of what a church should *not* be. He said, "I could not address you as spiritual but as worldly—mere infants in Christ. I gave you milk, not solid food, for you were not yet ready for it. Indeed, you are still not ready. You are still worldly. For since there is jealousy and quarreling among you, are you not worldly? Are you not acting like mere men? For when one says, 'I follow Paul,' and another, 'I follow Apollos,' are you not mere men?" What Paul is saying is this: In the church of Jesus Christ, we can respond to situations in a spiritually immature way, a "worldly way"; that is, a purely secular reaction to a spiritual situation.

Paul says that if we respond to these emphases or particular concerns in a secular way or in an inadequate spiritual way, the result is going to be all kinds of upset and strife. And this, of course, showed itself particularly in the church of Corinth. The people, instead of addressing the problems they were confronting, began to attack the people identified with the problems. One of the surest signs that the church is having difficulty is when personalities, rather than the problem, are attacked.

This is what was happening in the church of Corinth, in the church of Ephesus, and in the church of Crete, so it should come as no surprise if it therefore happens in the church today, anywhere on the face of God's earth. These attacks are the precursor to a division.

The situation escalates

Paul then uses an even stronger word. He says you have "foolish controversies and genealogies and arguments and quarrels about the law." The word *quarrel* is simply the word for "fight." A good old knock-down-drag-out church fight. And *fight* is related to the word for "sword." When swords are drawn, it is an utter disgrace to the church of Jesus Christ.

Why Are There Divisions?

Let's back up a little and see how these fights come about. There are three words to notice: *difference, difficulty,* and *division.* I believe with all my heart that differences are inevitable in the church of Jesus Christ. And because this is true, there is a high probability the church will run into difficulties, making divisions possible.

What is a division? A difficulty handled improperly. You say, "Well, let's get rid of all the difficulties." How are you going to do that? I'll tell you: Get rid of all the people. If you don't want the probability of difficulty, and if you don't want the possibility of division, there's only one way to handle it, and that is to empty the church of people.

But, you see, we can't do that. Instead, let's stick with the people. Let's accept that there will be differences; there will be difficulties. But let's make absolutely certain that in the differences and the difficulties, division is never allowed to raise its ugly head.

Differences are inevitable

Why will there be differences in the Church of Jesus Christ?

First, there are wide differences in scriptural knowledge. In the church of Jesus Christ, some people will speak with tremendous authority on a subject even though they have never even cracked a Bible. On the other hand, some people have studied carefully and assiduously. They will address a situation from a totally different perspective. The person who studied Scripture doesn't necessarily have all the answers nor is he necessarily always right. And the person who has not studied Scripture isn't necessarily always wrong. But what Paul points out is this: When you have differences in scriptural knowledge, you have people addressing an issue from totally different vantage points. Let's face it, there are some people who don't know much about the Bible, but they are gifted with good old common sense.

Let's thank God for people who have common sense. It would be marvelous if these people with common sense could take the trouble to find out what God says in his Word.

It is equally probable that you will come across people who have really studied God's Word, but they haven't brought much common sense to bear on it. Perhaps they have studied one aspect of the Bible but have never taken the time to balance it out with other aspects. So, accordingly, on the point of scriptural knowledge, there will be all kinds of difference.

Second, there are all kinds of differences in spiritual experience. Some people in the Christian church are babes in Christ. That is not a criticism; it happens to be a statement of fact. They have relatively recently come to know Christ as Savior and Lord. And their experience of him is fresh, delightful, and exciting, but by no stretch of the imagination mature.

On the other hand, some people in Christ are desperately mature and desperately dull—there's no sign of excitement. The freshness is long gone, and they exemplify the stereotypical church in many people's eyes. A lot of people who are spiritually mature are cold and correct, decorous and dead. A lot of people who are spiritual babes are warm and fresh and exciting, but they don't know what they're talking about. When you put them together you have the possibility of all kinds of differences.

Third, there are differences in social graces. There are some people who can handle a discussion and others who can't. Some people can sit down and talk, bring out their differences, and in the end shake hands and agree that neither of them has all the truth and neither of them has assimilated and accumulated all the facts; therefore, probably the sensible thing to do is to agree to disagree. But there are some people who can't do that, or won't do it. Every little point becomes an issue, every issue becomes a fight, every fight becomes a disaster, and they have one long history of total chaos.

Then, of course, there are differences of psychological makeup. Some people really like to have every *i* dotted and every *t* crossed because they feel very uncomfortable if there is any room for flexing. Other people feel totally throttled if there is no room for flexing. The people who want every *i* dotted and every *t* crossed are careful, detail-conscious, earnest people indeed. And when they bring this attitude to Christianity, they want chapter and verse for everything. They will stick their fingers in the Bible and say, "Show me where it is."

On the other hand, there are people who are more relaxed about the whole thing. They will say, "Listen, I can't give you chapter or verse, but there's no question about it. The general principle is there somewhere between Genesis and Revelation."

When a church has people with different psychological makeups, what happens? Some people, when a difference comes up, are desperately threatened by it. Others, when they come up against threatened people, are unbelievably frustrated with them. This is all it takes to produce all kinds of difference in the church which, if you're not careful, will begin to produce a difficulty.

Difficulties are probable

First of all, difficulties come about because *positions are not clear.* I think we've got to face up to one simple thing: People don't necessarily say what they mean. That is something in which I take great comfort. I certainly hope a lot of things people have said to me were not really what they meant!

There's another thing that we have to face up to, and it is that people don't necessarily hear what you say. And if they don't necessarily hear what you say and don't say what they mean, you have all kinds of possibilities, because people's positions may not be very clear at all by the time they have expressed themselves badly or listened inadequately.

As a result, *perspectives become clouded* as they begin to zero in on this particular issue. They spend more time talking about the issue and, in the end, forget why they are here. We get so wrapped up in the trees that we forget that there are woods and forests on every hand. And that makes a total clouding of the church's perspective very possible indeed.

Then, third, *personalities become involved*. One of the tragic things that happens when differences have been made into difficulties is that personalities become involved. People, not having expressed themselves properly or not having been heard adequately, sometimes begin to attribute motives to those related to the problem. That is one of the most dangerous things that can happen. It is one thing to say, "This is the problem." But when we lose sight of the problem and say, *"He* is the problem," that is serious.

The situation is made worse when people add, "He is the problem because this is what he is really doing and thinking." By then we have put the issue up so many notches that we are in real trouble. When personalities become involved, and when motives— almost invariably bad motives—are attributed to the personalities involved then you have the fourth problem: *Parties are formed*.

In Corinth, parties had developed around the powerful personalities. There was the Apollos party, the Peter party, the Paul party, and then the super saints, who said, "We're just Christ's people." This is when you have real trouble, because not only are people not hearing and expressing properly, but now they are arbitrarily identifying the motives of the personalities concerned and forming parties around those people. And before you know what's happened, all the energy of the church is spent in parties combating other parties.

Divisions are possible

When a church gets to the place where parties have been formed, there's a strong possibility that the diverse point in which they were interested becomes more important then the unity of the body. In other words, in the same way that in the political realm we tend towards single-issue voting, it is possible that in the church of Jesus Christ people can produce single-issue reactions. And when these are produced, the people are no longer interested in the body as a whole. They are no longer interested in the balanced life of the fellowship as a whole. Their sole concern is the issue. When this divisive issue becomes more important to them than the unity and life of the whole body, then the easiest thing in the world is for that person or that group to break off. That's serious.

There's another factor. Sometimes when we get into these situations, egos become involved, then pride becomes involved, and statements are made that cannot be retracted. We have taken a position from which we cannot move; we've gone out on a limb and we've sawed it off. And because there's no way back, we just decide, *I'm going to keep my pride and my ego intact and take whoever will come with me because my individual pride matters more than the corporate good.*

When this happens, the apostle Paul tells Titus: "Avoid foolish controversies and genealogies and arguments and quarrels about the law, because these are unprofitable and useless. Warn a divisive person once, and then warn him a second time. After that, have nothing to do with him. You may be sure that such a man is warped and sinful; he is self-condemned" (vv. 9-11).

Why Are Divisions Anathema?

Anathema is a Greek word that means something is "utterly condemned, totally unacceptable." Why do we use such a strong word as anathema about a division? For a number of reasons:

Christ's body is amputated

If you identify with a body of believers and then choose to be part of a division in that body, you are inflicting an *amputation* on that body. That's why you should always be careful before you leave a church; that's why you should always be careful before you join a church.

There is a difference between leaving a church in anger and leaving a church over an issue and joining with a group of people to establish a new church. I would call that an organ transplant. There is all the difference in the world between callously amputating a limb and generously donating a member. I believe the latter is permissible and necessary. I believe the former is out of order. The anathema of a division is that the body of Christ suffers amputation.

Christ's cause is misrepresented

We have plenty of people out there who are ready to be critical about Christians and about the church of Jesus Christ. Lots of people will have nothing to do with the church because of our sad history at this particular level. And we have given them all kinds of opportunities to misunderstand who Christ is, what his church is, and what Christians stand for. We should be careful before we ever give our critics opportunity to find fault with us.

Christ's disciples are humiliated

When it comes down to a fight, unfortunately, somebody wins and somebody loses. But in fact, the church of Jesus Christ loses all around. Why? Because those who win may feel totally justified in the way they handled matters. And those who lose are going to go away hurt, and possibly embittered. There's a real possibility that it's going to take them a long time to get over it. But, remember, they are still members of the body of Christ. That is why the apostle Paul says to be very careful about this whole business of division in the church.

I'd like to give you one example. In 1983 I was asked by *Moody Monthly* to write an article addressing the issue of whether it is possible that the gifts of women are being buried in the church of Jesus Christ. I said I thought it was a very real possibility and wrote an article accordingly. The article, in turn, generated a number of letters to the editor. Here's a sampling. One man wrote, "In regard to Stuart Briscoe's article, *nonsense.*" A lady wrote, "After reading several of your articles on the role of women, I was so infuriated, I had to sit down and write immediately. Please cancel my subscription."

The fascinating point, however, is that, although they both disagreed strongly with what I had written, they were taking exactly opposite positions.

The difficulty here stems from the differences of approach. Let's face it, there are some people who haven't cracked the Bible on this issue at all. There are some people in the church of Jesus Christ who address the issue of women in the church on a 100-percent secular basis. And they aren't feminists. Now, I understand feminists and have some degree of sympathy for some of *what* they are saying. I don't very often have too much sympathy for the *way* they're saying it, however.

But when people begin to address the specific issues of the church from a purely secular approach, we've got to accept the fact that, with all due respect, they may have some degree of truth, but they're really not addressing the issue. On the other hand, some people can stub their fingers in a verse and say, "It says here, 'Let the women keep silence' (see 1 Cor. 14:34). That's all there is to it." That is not all there is to it, because the same person who wrote, "Let the women keep silence" also explained under what circumstances they were allowed to break their silence. And he also had women who worked with him, of whom he approved, who did anything but keep silence.

Some people can take a verse and underline it until it comes through on the backside of the page. They've got their position. That's it. Other people will take this verse and that verse and pull the whole thing together, and you know what they'll discover? They'll discover that this thing is far more complex than they ever thought.

In fact, I would have to say, I believe the gospel of Jesus Christ is fundamentally simple and intrinsically complex. And, quite frankly, the more I study the Word of God, the less dogmatic I'm prepared to be on many issues.

If we have differences in approach, differences in psychological reactions to these things, let's face up to it. It's fascinating being a member of the church of Jesus Christ, because you've always got differences. If you're not careful, they'll produce difficulties, and if difficulties aren't handled properly, you finish up with a division.

Why Church Discipline Must Not Be Avoided

There have been times in church history when discipline has been exercised with something resembling fiendish delight. We have all been made aware by the critics of Christianity of some of our forebearers' excesses in the administration of church discipline. Burnings at the stake, wearing of scarlet letters, inquisitions have all served to make modern church people decidedly nervous about disciplining their members.

In more recent times the threat of legal action in the courts and the possible resultant crippling damages have made church leaders even more reluctant to deal with their erring members. But the fact remains that if proper discipline is not applied where appropriate, the result will be a marked decline in the spiritual nature of the church and a confusing signal for those who are trying to evaluate the pros and cons of religious experience. Then, of course, there's the loss suffered by the erring believers if they are never taken to task for their behavior, with restoration in mind.

When is discipline necessary?

There are at least three answers to this question.

First, *when people disrupt the building of the body.* There are times when members of a congregation, for whatever reason, seem to apply themselves to the tearing down of what other people are trying to build in the name of Christ. They should be dealt with patiently and carefully with a view to understanding why they are behaving in such a manner. But these kinds of people can demand far more attention than is their due, and the time will eventually come when the leaders of the church determine how much more attention can and should be given to the people concerned before they are presented with some straightforward alternatives. This kind of discipline requires great tact and insight, because while we should always be mindful of the individuals, we must also have in mind the well-being of the body as a whole.

Second, *when practices corrupt the life of the body.* There appear to be an increasing number of cases where people in the church have been ensnared in immoral situations in their businesses or their private sexual lives. This kind of situation is deeply embarrassing to all concerned, and as a result the natural tendency is to hope it isn't true and, if it is, to assume that it will go away. The problem with this approach is that when a member of the body engages in overtly immoral behavior, the reputation of the fellowship is inevitably tarnished, and, of course, the enemies of Christ are given yet another opportunity to blaspheme his name. Therefore, the old blind-eye approach is not good enough, and decisive and caring action must be taken.

Third, *when problems interrupt the ministry of the church.* It was Paul who admonished all believers to live at peace with each other (Rom. 12:18), but it was also he who confronted Peter concerning his problematic behavior (Gal. 2:11). Was he being self-contradictory? No, there came a time in Paul's estimation when living at peace with Peter became secondary to ensuring that the work of the ministry went unhindered. When in his judgment that time arrived, he stepped into the situation and the sparks began to fly, although it should be pointed out that the two men apparently remained on good terms after the confrontation. In all ministries there is the possibility that similar decisions will need to be made, but, like all disciplinary issues, they are by no means easy, and require the greatest of care.

How is discipline administered?

The people concerned are approached personally. This needs to be stressed because it is far easier to approach someone else rather than the offending person. The intent in the approach is, of course, to "warn" the person, presumably about the seriousness of the behavior and possibly with a view to outlining the perceived consequences of what has transpired. This instruction would be designed presumably to outline a series of steps that would be appropriate to remedy the situation, but at the same time there would be a serious statement concerning the necessity for action to be taken by the fellowship if the proposed remedies are ignored or disregarded. If appropriate responses are forthcoming, then reconciliation can begin, but if nothing is achieved, then what?

The people concerned are approached again. These instructions should, of course, be read in conjunction with the well-known teaching of our Lord recorded in Matthew 18:15-20. If the pastoral instructions are harmonized with Jesus' teachings, the return visit would presumably be conducted in the presence of others who are aware of the problem and who care deeply for the offending people and those who are being offended. It is always hoped at this juncture that if the initial visit was fruitless, then the second visit will not only show the depth of concern of the church leaders, but will also show, by the fuller participation of others, that this is a matter to be taken with the utmost seriousness. But what if there is still no response?

The people concerned are disciplined. The discipline Titus is required to administer is related to a brand of social ostracism, which would be deeply humiliating and devastating in the days of the early church, even more so than at the present time. In those days there would not be a church on every street corner in most of the Cretan towns, so if the disciplined person was "avoided" and the members of the fellowship "had nothing to do with them," it would be a great disgrace.

Today people often fail to respond in repentance to admonitions, but compound the problem by denying what they have done and simply transfer to another church, which more often than not is not at all interested in why they are no longer attending their previous fellowship. Added to this are the dark threats of legal action. All in all, a sad state of affairs exists in the modern church when disciplinary action is attempted. However, this does not mean it should be abandoned, because there are always cases of people who, when they are treated firmly and lovingly, do respond and as a result come through the experience richer and more mature. The same can also be said for the church and its leadership when they have sought to discipline properly with a view to honoring the name of Christ, preserving the integrity of the fellowship, and seeking to lead the erring one into a deeper knowledge of the Lord.

In the church there is no shortage of hot heads and cold hearts, and these do not adorn the gospel. We need cool heads and warm hearts if the church is to be disciplined in order to be discipled.

I would prefer not to end this book on such a note. No one wishes to concentrate on division in the church, its causes and potential cures. Nevertheless if the church is to be recognizably "the people of God" whom God is purifying for himself it stands to reason that those whose lives militate against God's purposes must be dealt with for the honor of God's name and the well-being of God's people.

With this in mind may I encourage you, my reader, to take seriously the exalted view of the local church so powerfully expounded by Paul to Titus. And may I urge you to be a means, like Titus, through whom God's glorious purposes for the church are fulfilled.

Making It Real

1. How do divisions in the church come about?

2. What are some of the areas on which the church is divided today? How can we exhibit unity despite differences in these areas?

3. Why must we be strict in dealing with division in the church?

4. How and when should discipline in the church be carried out?